*What others are saying about Theo's Stand...*

"*Theo's Stand* is a fresh look at one of the most compelling passages in the Bible: the armor of God. With fresh insight and through the intrigue of story, Hagel has created an action-packed study that will challenge the reader to dig deeper in their walk with God."
— Tara Johnson, author of *To Speak His Name*

"Creative and engaging, this book is sure to equip and strengthen believers for the daily fight, as well as to give assurance of final victory. I highly recommend it!"
— Ann Tatlock, novelist, editor, writing mentor

"Hagel's authentic voice invites young believers to explore discipleship deeply and find grounding in today's shifting culture. This study is a powerful resource, inspiring faith and resilience for a new generation."
— John Herring, CEO, Iron Stream Media

"Here is a compelling study, for which I could chew on over and over again!...Charisa Hagel not only reminds us of our daily and potentially destructive battle with Satan, but she offers solid biblical evidence in combination with the powerful story of *Theo's Stand* to guide us to victory."
—Dr. Jean-Noel Thompson, Ph.D., Executive Vice President at Harding University, and personal friend of Charisa's

# THEO'S STAND

A personal study on the armor of God
-Time to Fight Series-
Charisa Hagel

THEO'S STAND: A personal study on the armor of God
-Time to Fight Series-

Copyright © 2025 by Charisa Hagel

All rights reserved.

Unless otherwise noted, all Scripture quotations are taken from the New King James Version of the Bible. Copyright © 1982 by Thomas Nelson, Inc., publishers. Used by permission. All rights reserved.

No portion of this book may be reproduced in any form without written permission from the publisher or author, except as permitted by U.S. copyright law.

Cover Design: Dolan Trout
Editor: Michael White

ISBN: 979-8-9926521-0-9 (paperback)
ISBN: 979-8-9926521-1-6 (digital)

This book is dedicated to the work of the Lord, for without Him, none of this would be possible. To God be the glory—now and forever.

To the reader of this book, I pray the Holy Spirit stirs in you the desire to take a stand against spiritual darkness, to fight the good fight of faith, to stand when you feel like falling, to kneel when hope seems lost, and to rely solely upon the One who gives you the strength to endure, so that when the battle is won, you may give praise to the Father and Son, Jesus Christ, our Lord, who has gone before you and made a way when there seemed to be no way.

# Contents

| | |
|---|---:|
| Prologue | 1 |
| We are Chosen | 23 |
| Be Strong | 30 |
| Wiles of the Devil | 34 |
| Physical and Spiritual Battles | 39 |
| Standing Ready | 48 |
| The Belt of Truth | 57 |
| The Breastplate of Righteousness | 74 |
| The Shoes of Preparation and Peace | 86 |
| The Shield of Faith | 98 |
| The Helmet of Salvation | 109 |
| The Sword of The Spirit | 119 |
| Praying Always | 133 |
| Being Bold | 139 |
| Choosing to Fight | 143 |
| Epilogue | 150 |

| | |
|---|---|
| Acknowledgments | 152 |
| About the Author | 154 |
| Endnotes | 155 |

# Prologue

A knock penetrated Theo's thoughts. *Who was that?* He stood in the watchtower, listening. Nothing.

Shaking his head, he turned and watched the enemy outside. For days raiding parties had been coming in, and now hundreds of men marched in the field nearby, practiced archery, and struck sword against sword. The sound of their shouts and banter filled his ears. Their red and black banners sliced through the wind like a knife through flesh. The campfires burned with embers of bright orange, and the dark smoke cast haunting figures in the sky. Their taunting echoed across the plains, and when they chanted, it sent shivers down Theo's spine. *How long could he avoid the fight that was to come, and how long would he be safe within the walls of his castle?*

Another knock was heard, followed by the pounding of a fist against wood. The sound continued as he left the tower and moved to the East gate.

"Who is there?" he shouted and then listened for a reply.

"A messenger from the King of the Highlands. Do not fear," a voice responded.

Pulling open a small peep hole attached to the door, Theo observed a man dressed in the King's colors. His cloak was a dark purple, trimmed in gold, with a lion embroidered on the chest. Unbolting the gate's door, he welcomed the man inside.

"The King received your message," the messenger relayed. "I have come to aid you, and reinforcements are on their way."

Looking from the messenger to the black smoke clouding the sky from the enemy's campfires, Theo shook his head. "We are two against a whole army. No! There is no chance we will survive. I need help *now*!" He ran a hand through his hair and rubbed the back of his neck. Beads of sweat rolled down his face.

"I *am* your help," the messenger reassured him, "The King wants you to hold the enemy off until the reinforcements arrive."

"What?! How can I do that?" Theo's eyes grew wide, and he shook his head. Grabbing the handle of the dagger hanging from his belt, he added in a shaky voice, "All I have is this knife."

"Did not the King give you an armory within this castle?" the messenger asked.

"I think so. . . .Yes, but I never go in there."

"It is time you do. Show me where it is."

Theo led the messenger across the brick courtyard and into a stone building next to the stables. It was barely visible in the morning light. Theo's castle, like many others, was small and stood on the border of the land. It was surrounded with high stone walls for fortification. Inside the armory, the interior was covered with various types of weapons. Theo stared, eyes widening as he surveyed the walls. Shields and swords—arrayed in X shapes—hung everywhere. *Had these always been here? When were all these weapons to be used?*

"Now, you have just recently finished your training, and this castle is your first assignment. Correct?" the messenger asked as he walked in behind him.

Theo nodded, still absorbing all the battle equipment around him. "Yes. After I pledged allegiance to the King, I was given this castle to guard."

"Good," the messenger bobbed his head and walked toward a shelf full of chain mail, metal helmets, and shoes.

Theo continued, "That was right before the King of the Lowlands laid siege and, as you must have seen when you came, camped around the castle.

They have been sending threats for days now. I sent messages entreating the King to send me aid and to save me." Theo looked at the messenger. "How did you get past them?"

"We must get ready," the messenger instructed, ignoring his question.

Lifting a sword off the wall, Theo declared, "I am ready!"

The messenger shook his head. "A sword is good, but you need protection. The first thing is armor. Different fights require different weapons, but *all* fights require armor."

Collecting the articles of metal from the shelf, the messenger stood before Theo. "It is my duty to prepare you for war. As I suit you up, I will explain each piece of armor and its purpose."

Theo nodded, and the messenger began with a tunic of small chains.

"The chain mail encompasses you and is your first layer of protection. It is like a padding between you and everything else. It is also used to deflect oncoming blows."

"Then if I wear this, I will not get hurt?" Theo inquired.

"No," the messenger said, "It does not make you invincible. It guards you. Some attacks will penetrate it, but it will lessen the damage of the blow." Having put the tunic on him, the messenger reached for a large belt. "This belt holds all the other pieces together. We must take care to properly fix it in place. It holds your sword, and with the belt properly secured around you, it allows for the quickest access to your weapon."

Theo sheathed the sword and then quickly drew it out again. "*That* was easy."

"In the armory, where we are safe and have no fear, it is easy, but the test will come when you are outside facing the enemy. The steps to retrieve your sword are the same, but the enemy will try to dissuade you from using it. It is vital that you know where your sword is, so when the enemy is upon you, you can act quickly and not miss."

Theo swallowed hard. His thoughts turned to the enemy beyond the wall.

"This breastplate is to protect your heart and chest," the messenger continued, "which is the largest and most common target of the enemy. If he can pierce your heart, he has won. Weakening you is to his advantage, but killing you is his goal."

Theo touched the breastplate over his chest as the messenger tightly secured it.

"The breastplate also overlaps the belt giving further protection and still allowing access to your sword." Reaching down, the messenger lifted a pair of shoes. "These shoes are to protect your feet so when you walk, your feet will not be pierced by fallen arrows or weapons as they drop during the fight. The small spikes on the bottom of the foot allow you to grip the earth and stand firm. They can also be used during the fight for further protection." He knelt and fastened the shoes on Theo's feet. Walking to the nearest wall, the messenger lifted a large rectangular shield.

Theo's eyes brightened. "*That* will protect me."

"Yes, it will, but you must hold onto it. As with all the pieces, this shield is a vital piece of the armor, but do not be deceived. It is heavier and stronger than one perceives. This will help you in the battle, but at times you may grow weary. Do not let go. Do not doubt or give up. This shield is to guard your entire being, or that of another. Its size and rectangular shape allow complete coverage when you kneel. It will also enable you to walk boldly before the enemy."

As he placed it in Theo's hand, a grunt escaped Theo's lips as he felt the weight of the shield.

"The helmet is to guard your head and neck." The messenger explained as he set it on Theo's head. "Even though it protects you physically, you still must mentally block out the voice of the enemy. Do you understand?"

Theo looked into the messenger's eyes. There was a severity and determination deep within which required an answer. Theo nodded.

The messenger stared one moment longer and moved on. "The enemy must not enter your mind, for if he does, he will cause you to stumble, leading to total destruction of your mind and body. Now the sword, your dagger," the messenger pointed to the weapon sheathed on Theo's belt. "This is to defend yourself from the enemy when he is at close range."

"How close is close range?" Theo asked with a tremor in his voice.

"At some point," the messenger said, "we must fight hand-to-hand combat—but do not be afraid. We are to be prepared and ready. We must know what to do and how to act when wielding this powerful weapon."

Theo blew air from between his lips. *There is so much to learn.* But he determined to do it.

Looking around the room, the messenger walked to a pile of bows and arrows. Retrieving some, he returned to Theo. "Each battle calls for its own weapon. If you are unsure what that weapon may be, this is always a good one to start with. It is powerful and effective. Have you ever used one before?"

"Yes. On occasion," Theo answered as he reached for the extended bow and quiver of arrows.

"If you use the bow and arrow properly," the messenger said, "it reaches its target at a great distance while protecting you with that same distance. Come. I will show you." With his own bow and arrows in hand, he left the armory, and Theo followed.

In the courtyard, the messenger set up a plank of wood as a target. Instructing Theo to follow his lead, he strung his bow, set the arrow, pulled back, and released. The arrow struck the target in the center.

Theo raised his bow, set his arrow, pulled back, and released. The arrow nipped the edge of the target as it flew past. Theo growled.

The messenger nodded. "You need to strengthen your stance."

"What do you mean?" Theo turned to look at him.

The messenger came and stood beside him. "Like this," he stood with his left shoulder towards the target and his feet apart. "You need to make certain your stance can hold and balance you." He leaned forward, backward, and to the sides but kept his feet firmly planted. "Now tighten your arms and turn your face toward the target."

Theo did as he was instructed.

"Good. The position of your stance will aid you in your aim. For your arrows to be most effective, your stance must be firm, your arms must be strong, and your eyes must be focused. Do not look away from it. If you look away and release the arrow, the arrow will follow the direction of your eyes and arms, and it will cause your aim to be off. Try again."

Theo planted his feet, and then placed the arrow against the bow and on the string.

"Shoulders back," the messenger instructed; "pull to the corner of your mouth and keep your eyes on the target."

Theo nodded.

"And take a deep breath," the messenger added.

Theo breathed in, focused on the target, and breathed out.

"And release."

Theo did, and the arrow flew from his bow and struck the target in the left upper corner. He turned to the messenger. "I missed the center."

The messenger smiled, "But you hit the target. Accuracy will come with practice. Adjust your aim by moving your arms slightly lower and keep them firm when you release.

For the next several days, the messenger instructed Theo on how to shoot, fight, and guard himself with his armor. While Theo grew tired and his muscles ached, the smoke from the enemy camp and the messenger's encouragement to stand strong against the highly trained soldiers kept him going.

The messenger reminded him, "You are going against professionals. It is vital to keep your mind and weapons ready and sharp. Let us practice again."

One day, as the heat of the sun bore down on them, Theo and the messenger stopped their sword practice for a drink of water. Out of breath, Theo asked, "What happened?"

"To what?" the messenger inquired as he lifted a jar of water to his lips.

"To cause the war. Why do we have to fight? All I know is that it has been going on since before I was born."

The messenger looked up at the enemy banners waving beyond the castle walls. "Mondos was once a place of peace governed by the King of the Highlands," the messenger began. Deep shadows clouded his eyes as a memory arose in his mind.

He was silent so long that Theo spoke up, "Sir?"

The messenger shook his head, breaking the trance, and continued, "A commander within the ranks rose up and fought against our Sovereign. He started a rebellion and declared himself King. A third of the army swore their allegiance to him. For their treachery, they were banished from the kingdom. When he was cast out, he and those who followed him settled in the lowlands. Since that time, war has plagued the land. The banished commander, who you know as the King of the Lowlands, is always tormenting the servants faithful to the true King. He is relentless in his attacks, aiming to destroy all who stand in his way. Why do we fight? Because evil and good war against one another. The darkness will always hate and fight the light. We fight to keep the light. We fight for what is true. We fight because we stand with the true King. And as long as the enemy seeks his own glory, there will always be war. For there is only one King."

"You must be careful of your surroundings, soldier," the messenger cautioned him. "The enemy prowls around like a lion, seeking who he can devour. But come," the messenger stood, stretching his arms and back. "Let us practice again. There is a time and season for all things, but during a battle is not the time for rest or sleep but for action. Rest will come later."

As the messenger and Theo practiced, they heard knocking at the South gate. They approached the door and opened the small hole to see who was there. A man dressed in a dusty gray tunic stood asking to be let in. His sleeves were ripped and tattered and mud caked his hands and feet.

"Please," he called out, "the enemy is everywhere. Please, save me, and let me in."

Theo reached to remove the crossbar when the messenger placed a hand on his arm, stopping him.

"We cannot let just anyone into the castle," the messenger whispered. "Everyone must be tested." Calling out through the opening he asked, "From where do you come?"

"A place far from here," the man replied. "I have traveled so long. I'm starving and tired. Please, oh, please, let me in!"

Theo turned to the messenger. "Shall I let him in?"

The messenger shook his head. "I have an ill feeling. Something is not right concerning this man. Let us wait to see what occurs. Tell him we will drop him a basket of food from the wall, but we cannot let him enter."

Theo did as the messenger instructed.

That night, the messenger stood guard on the wall. He watched the stranger beneath but remained out of the line of sight.

The man looked at the bread, scoffed, and tossed it aside. With the cover of night, he headed toward the enemy camp.

Waking Theo, the messenger directed his attention to the stranger sneaking toward the camp. "He was one of theirs."

"The skunk! That lying snake!" Theo spat out.

"Lying and deceiving is what the enemy does." The messenger added, "If he can trick you to let him in without a fight, he's won. Nothing is beneath him. He is not a noble opponent. He will employ any tactic to take you down. They know now that the only way in is to break through the fortress walls. They will go for the weakest point in the structure." The messenger pointed to the wall across from them. "There is where they will come through, for there the bricks are not as strong."

Taking a deep breath, Theo asked, "Is there nothing we can do to stop it?"

A small smile formed on the messenger's lips. He placed a hand on Theo's shoulder. "We can strengthen that which remains. Physically, let us gather whatever we can find to fortify and create an inner-like wall. Mentally, let us strengthen our hearts and prepare our minds. The fight is coming."

Theo and the messenger started that night fortifying the wall. Piling up unused bricks, boards, and sacks of grain, they alternated between standing guard and construction.

"We will never make it as high as the other wall," Theo sighed.

The messenger wiped his brow with the back of his arm. "We do not have to match the height. The inner wall is not to replace the outer wall, but to strengthen it and to hinder the enemy." Rolling his head to the sides and massaging his muscles, the messenger looked at Theo. "Let me tell you of a time of our ancestors. A once glorious city had been destroyed, brought to heaps of ash. But one soldier, with great faith and dedication, began to rebuild. With a blessing from the King, he gathered all those who had been scattered and invited them to join him in construction. But, like you, the enemy saw and drew near. Aware of his surroundings, this brave soldier equipped all the citizens with weapons to fight. However, they were instructed not to stop building. So, while they waited, armed for an attack, they strengthened and rebuilt the wall, brick by brick. The enemy scoffed at first and laughed, believing them to have undertaken an impossible feat. He thought they would never finish such a task, but they did. And because they were ready and did not waiver in their commitment to finish, they were able to raise the city walls faster than anyone thought possible. So let us take heart and not give up or grow weary. Let us be like those before us, working with one hand and armed in the other."

Theo agreed and bent down, reaching for another board to add to the wall.

For days they toiled hard but did not stop. Outside the wall they could hear the enemy shouting orders and building their own device. Glancing at one another, they each took a deep breath. The enemy could attack at any moment, and they had to be ready.

---

As the sun rose above the horizon, bringing streaks of pink and gold above them, Theo took a deep breath. They had finished their construction, and the time was near. He looked around for the messenger and saw him down on bended knee. His head rested in the palm of his hand with the elbow against his knee.

The messenger looked up as Theo approached.

"We have strengthened the wall," Theo said as he shook his head. "But how do I strengthen my heart? I do not feel ready."

"Then let me encourage you. You have been given everything you need to face this battle. Do not be afraid." The messenger looked toward the newly built wall. "War is not just physical. We must set our minds and focus. We put aside fears and doubts. We pray, as I have done. And we make the choice within ourselves to stand against the enemy. The fight will not be easy, but we can overcome them. Have no fear."

Nodding, Theo followed the messenger's lead and knelt.

Within the hour, the enemy formed into ranks and advanced. The sound of drums and marching soldiers filled the air. Carrying a battering ram with them, they approached the wall. The fight had begun.

---

Theo and the messenger, like two soldiers, stood in the watchtower with their armor on and their minds ready. Loading their arrows and pulling back the bow strings, the two aimed at the enemy. Releasing their hold, the arrows flew and struck the targets.

"Again," the messenger commanded.

They reloaded and let their arrows fly. They continued shooting as new soldiers replaced the dead. Theo's arms grew tired, but he could not stop. His heartbeat pounded against his chest like the drums of war. The danger of death was before him, and there was no stopping. As the enemy pounded against the wall, the bricks and mortar began to shake. Bits of the wall were chipped away with each hit of the battering ram.

"Keep shooting!" the messenger shouted as he released his arrow. "Aim for those closest and those beside the battering ram. Force them away from the wall!"

They shot those near the castle, but it did not stop the assault. The thundering and pounding of the wall did not cease.

The sun shifted positions in the sky above, declaring each passing hour.

"They will break through in a matter of moments! Get down! We will continue this fight from the ground," the messenger called as the floor beneath them shook once more.

"But is it not safer up here?"

"Not once they breach the wall. Come. We must be ready for their entry and assault."

As Theo followed the messenger, his head swirled and his stomach grew tight while the air grew thick with dust. Stepping into the courtyard, his eyes darted to the cracking wall. The shouts of the enemy pounded in his head. His heart was beating like thunder in his chest. His mind raced with stories of ancient battles where thousands of the King's men had fallen. He shook his head, longing to displace the thoughts, willing his mind to focus on what lay ahead. The messenger's voice penetrated the chaos in his mind.

"The moment they break through, we release the arrows. It will give us a little more time before they are upon us," the messenger explained as he readied his bow. "Now, take your stand."

Theo loaded his bow once more.

With his bow strung, he waited. Each second seemed an eternity as bits of brick and mortar flew into the air. A pounding thud shook the structure. The very ground quaked beneath the attack. The sound of cracking stones echoed in the air. Again and again, the castle shuddered and seemed to moan with each hit. Suddenly, with a shattering of brick and stone, the wall fell, caving in, and creating a path for the enemy to enter. As dust rose from the crumbled wall, Theo and the messenger released their arrows causing the intruding foes to fall. The next line of attacking soldiers crawled over their fallen comrades and pushed their way through the rubble, but they were slowed down by the inner wall, giving Theo and the messenger an advantage of a few more seconds. But they entered the courtyard all too soon. They were clad in black armor with a multi-headed dragon etched in red on their chests and shields. The parts of their body not covered in armor held an unearthly appearance of black ash. Across their faces ran a red stain like the trailing of blood. Their chilling screams intensified their appearance as they raced forward. Several men threw torches and destroyed structures. Others ran straight for Theo and the messenger.

Releasing another arrow, the messenger shouted, "Prepare for close range fighting!"

Tightening his jaw, Theo narrowed his eyes at the invading enemy. Tossing aside his bow, he reached for his sword. As he unsheathed it, his hand shook. He squeezed his grip tighter, forcing his hand to remain in control. With his other hand, he retrieved his shield.

"Do not be afraid," the messenger cried as he took the large shield from his own back and placed it before him. Two enemy soldiers ran toward them screaming. The messenger slid his right foot back and waited. As they approached, he plunged forward smashing them with the front of his shield. The two stumbled back a step but kept their feet. Pulling out his sword, he slammed his shield into one and struck the other with his blade. They both fell. One limped off; the other died and hit the ground. Before the messenger was able to take a breath, two more foes took their comrades' places.

With heart racing, Theo faced his own foe. An enemy covered in black armor stood before him. Holding a large sword with jagged edges, the opponent swung it around himself like a madman. Carefully watching the enemy's movement, Theo was prepared for the coming strike and blocked it with his shield. The enemy attacked high and low, causing Theo to dodge, block, counter, or be hit. Theo spun around his foe and struck him in the back between his chain mail and breastplate. His attacker fell with a thud. Both triumph and fear surged through his body as he looked up from the fallen opponent to watch more approach. It felt like the enemy continued to flood through the opening like ants attacking from a smashed ant hill. His hands shook, unknowingly loosening the grip on his shield and sword. An opponent leapt in and slammed against his side. The jolt shook Theo from his thoughts and caused him to drop his shield. It fell to the ground. Miraculously, his sword was still in hand as he reeled to face the enemy. He managed to block the first strike but not the second one. He soon found himself cut across the arm and on the ground before his opponent. The enemy prepared for a final blow and raised his weapon. Seeing an opening, Theo thrust his blade into the foe, striking a deadly blow. His adversary fell to the ground. The horror and realization of what had just happened caused Theo's whole body to shake.

Unaware of his own danger, and still in shock, he remained on the ground as if frozen to it.

Across the courtyard, an enemy pulled back an arrow, aiming straight at Theo.

Seeing the present and future danger for his comrade, the messenger pushed off his own opponent with a blow that finished him and dashed over as protection. As the messenger ran in front, the arrow struck his shield, level with Theo's head.

Hearing the sound, Theo roused from his stupor and stared at the messenger.

"Praise the Lord!" came from the messenger's lips before he said, "Get up, boy! We are not finished. Pick up your shield, and do not lose faith. We are fully equipped to take them! Do not be afraid!" With quick movements, the messenger left his shield in front of Theo, sheathed his sword, picked up a fallen bow and arrow, drew an arrow, released, and struck the enemy who had attacked Theo. Dropping the bow, he reclaimed his shield and turned to Theo with an outstretched hand.

Theo gripped the messenger's hand and accepted the assistance.

Unsheathing his sword once more, the messenger instructed Theo again to pick up his shield.

Theo did as he was bidden and reclaimed his shield. He stood beside the messenger, ready to face the oncoming foes yet again.

---

They fought side by side all day and into the night. Darkness began to claim the atmosphere, and fog hovered over the battlefield and courtyard. Drops of rain battered their faces. With this cloak of nature, it became difficult to see. The air grew heavy weighing down those who were fighting. As tired and exhausted as Theo grew, the fighting remained as unyielding and consistent as before. However, by midnight, the enemy had regrouped outside the wall. The fog turned to moisture and landed on the earth.

"I am so tired," Theo murmured as he slid to the ground and leaned his head against the cold bricks of a nearby structure after putting out the fire the rain had not quenched.

Ripping off a strip of cloth from his tunic, the messenger knelt beside Theo and began to bind his wounds.

"Thank you for saving me," Theo said.

"You are welcome." The messenger tied the cloth and then asked, "When did you lose faith?"

"What do you mean?"

"When did you think it was too much?"

Theo stared at his arm, not wanting to look at his comrade or admit the truth.

"I saw your shield fall," the messenger continued and sat down beside him. "When it dropped it was as if you lost faith and gave up."

Theo nodded.

"You do know that you do not need to fear? Your shield can take the impact. Do not doubt it."

Theo looked up, "I do not think I doubted my shield but rather myself. I was not strong enough. The enemy caused it to fall from my hand with one unforeseen hit, and I did not hold on to it."

"Let me ask you something: Who is it that you are trusting to get you through this battle?"

Reflecting a moment, Theo answered, "I do not know. I suppose I was trusting my skill." He laughed. "Although it appears I do not have much of that."

"Your focus was in the wrong place. It was in your own power. If you lean on your own strength, it will not be strong enough, and you will fall."

Theo stared helplessly at his blistered hands while heaving a sigh. "But that is all I have. And you told me I had to hold off the enemy." Theo looked up at the messenger. His eyes were weary and tired.

The messenger sighed. "Your strength and skill are not all you have. It may be all you see, but it is not all that you have. You have been given wisdom, power, and authority. You have been given a strength that none can truly comprehend. A strength that does not come from you physically, but from within, and that enables you to do what you did today and fight a battle that, to the onlooker, seems impossible to win. However, when we try to do things in our own strength, that is when we fail. We must trust and stand in him who is stronger than ourselves. Man's flesh and power are not enough. We need the protection given to us by the King. Even though the King is not physically here with us, he is still protecting us. His protection allows us to face the unknown without fear and with an inner peace. It is his armor we wear and his sword we fight with. He is coming, and he will demolish the enemy. So put your trust not in yourself but in him who is able to do far more than we are able." He took a deep breath. "Now, get some sleep. I will take the first watch. You can have the second."

A few hours later, the messenger woke Theo for his watch and laid down for a rest. Theo walked back and forth, keeping his eyes trained for any enemy movement. As the time trickled by, his eyelids grew heavy. He stretched his legs, willing himself to stay alert. The shattered entrance still held no sign of any intruder. The minutes moved slowly like the small breeze that drifted through the dark night. Sitting down, he rubbed his tired legs and rested his chin against his chest. Soon, the exhausted eyelids shut, and he slept.

"Wake up!" the messenger roared.

Theo jerked awake to the alarm, fear grasping him as an enemy lurched forward. With hands outstretched, he grasped Theo's neck. A searing pain shot through Theo as he struggled to breathe.

Before the attacker finished his maneuver, the messenger's arm encircled the enemy's neck, and he rammed a dagger between the black armor and up into the chest. The dying foe loosened his grip and fell dead.

Theo gasped for breath and rubbed his hand over his bruised throat.

"Are you alright?" The messenger turned to Theo.

He nodded.

"We must stay alert. Never let your guard down," the messenger said. "You recover. I'll stand watch."

"Will they ever stop attacking?" Theo wheezed, still rubbing where the attacker grabbed him.

The messenger shook his head. "No. Not until they are completely destroyed. We have been blessed they broke for a respite and have not returned in full force. The enemy loves the darkness. He knows how well it covers him, and how tired we become. We must always be vigilant and alert."

With his head in his hands, Theo groaned. "Why is it I keep failing? I let my guard down on the battlefield. I dropped my shield, and now, I fell asleep and could have caused both of our deaths."

"Do not focus on the evil of what could have been. That guilt is a tactic of the enemy to get your mind off the battle at hand. Do not let him play with your mind. Let us learn from our mistakes and grow stronger. Do not focus on the fact that you failed or feel like a failure. Focus instead on what you can learn from failure and how you can grow stronger. Guilt holds you down, but conviction causes action and change. When we fall on the battlefield, do we stay down? By no means! If we did, we would be dead. We must immediately get back up and fight again. If you drop your shield, pick it back up. If you become afraid, remember you are never alone. Fear is also a tactic of the enemy, one which we are to overcome. We are not given a spirit of fear, but we are given power and a sound mind. If you grow tired, pray for strength, fight your flesh, and conquer the battle within yourself so you can fight the battles around you. If we are not totally in the battle, we leave that unconquered parcel of ourselves as ground to be overtaken and conquered by the enemy. He takes everything, even thoughts. It will be much harder to fight the enemy if he holds those places. Therefore, we must stand strong and not give up. We must endure to the end."

As the two talked, an arrow landed in the square. It had a piece of paper tied to it. Trying to remain alert, Theo looked around, grabbed a torch from the wall, and then retrieved the arrow and note.

*This fight is strenuous on everyone. Let us stop this unnecessary quarrel and pain. The King of the Highlands is not coming. Therefore, let us make a deal with you. Surrender the castle and yourselves, and we will have mercy. The boy may go his way in peace. Yet, if you refuse, we will attack with greater force than you can imagine. We will destroy everything. We will have no mercy. Your lives will be ours. And everything you hold dear will be burned. Remember, you are surrounded and cannot escape. You have until dawn to decide.*

The messenger read it and scoffed, "The mercy of the wicked is cruel. Never make a deal with the enemy. He offers an illusion of true peace, but it will never be. He might make it sound appealing, but do not believe him. He will dangle what you want, in your case the fighting to stop, and offer it to you on his terms, but know this: the enemy is a liar. He twists words of peace and devises traps for the subjects of the King. There is no peace where he is concerned. If you live by his terms, you will not live but surely die. In this note, he claims he will let you go, but he does not say when or how, or on what conditions, or that you will make it one mile before he strikes you from behind or shoots an arrow in your back." The messenger shook his head and stared out into the dark. "Let me tell you about a man who made a deal with the enemy. He was promised great wealth if he would sneak one enemy soldier into the fortified fortress where he lived. They only wanted him to get one man in. He consented. What harm could one soldier do? Caring more for the promised riches than the consequences, he played their evil game. Once he let the enemy in, the intruder rushed to the gate, killed the guard on duty, and opened it up, allowing the army to pour in. They slaughtered those within and set the city aflame. As agreed, the traitor was given great wealth—a room full of gold and silver—but he was trapped inside four walls without a window or door. His greatest desire ended up killing him. He could not eat the gold. He died surrounded by those riches he wanted so much—in a city of dead bodies he had helped to murder."

Theo tightened his fists. His chin contracted. "How could he betray his own people for gold? Traitor! He deserved the death he got." His voice burned with anger.

"There was another man," the messenger continued, "whose family was kidnapped by the enemy. He gathered an army to rescue them. Three weeks into the battle, he and his men prepared for another fight when he was given an ultimatum. The enemy told him they would release his family if he surrendered himself and his army. If he did not agree, they would hang his wife and children from the fortress wall for him to watch."

Theo's stomach tensed inside him.

The messenger went on, "Loving his family more than anything else, he agreed to the terms. The enemy approached his camp, and he surrendered, handing over all weapons. They bound him and took him to a high tower within their fortress. He was forced to watch as they slaughtered every man in his army. Closing his eyes, he tried to tell himself it was the only way to save his family. But the image of his murdered soldiers lying in their own blood remained. The field was covered with the dead. When the massacre ended, his captors dragged him down to the courtyard. There he saw his family. They had been beaten and tortured. Their faces looked like masks of blood shaded by swelling colors of black and blue. Their skin, like the color of death, was a sickening fusion of yellow and gray. Their clothes were torn in shreds, barely staying on. Their feet were like those of a skeleton. You could count each bone. They were only able to stand because of the guards forcing them there. He lurched forward in an effort to reach them, only to be pulled back and struck by the guard holding his chains. 'We just wanted you to see them before we let them free,' his captor taunted him, reminding him that he was not free, nor could he protect them. Dragging his family to the gate, the guards shoved them out. The wife reached for her children as they hit the ground. 'Wait!' the man called out. The enemy scoffed, 'Say goodbye.' Laughing, the captor raised his hand. The next moment arrows soared through the air and struck those he loved. 'No!' He screamed and tried to break from the enemy's hold, but he was unable. He fought with the chains binding his wrists. He attempted to push away the guard holding him captive. A searing pain throbbed through his knees as his captor struck him, causing him to collapse to the ground. A roar broke from his lungs at the physical agony combined with the agony of the heart that ripped him apart. Tears poured from his eyes as the cries of his loved ones burned his ears and soul. Then there was silence. 'No. No,' was all he could whisper. And all he could do was stare at the bodies of his beloved, arrows protruding out of them. One of the children's bodies still quivered. 'Put out his eyes,' came the command, and two soldiers held him down by his arms. He struggled, but in vain. The enemy held him firm. A glowing ember on the tip of an iron appeared before him. Suddenly, his eyes burned, and his flesh became like fire. As he thrashed about, the smell of his own body burning filled his nostrils. The pain did not stop as darkness invaded and overcame him. The laugh of the enemy pierced the atmosphere. He heard as they slammed the gate shut, shutting him in with them. His heart sank as the reality of his own choices hit him. He gained nothing in his agreement with the enemy. He had lost what he loved most and had thrown away not only his chance to fight, but the lives of all who fought with him."

The messenger turned away from the darkness and looked at Theo. "In many battles, the enemy holds ransom something we want or love dearly. But no matter the situation, we cannot compromise. Compromising is lethal. We must stand strong. Do not let the enemy get a foothold in your thoughts. He sends messages of fear or desire. He tries to play games with your mind. Stay alert. He is aiming to deter your mind from the fight. He wants to get you off balance—physically, mentally, and spiritually. If he can do that, it will be easier to sneak around you and attack." The messenger rose and reached for his sword. "No. We will **never** agree to his terms. Stay prepared. The battles do not stop until the enemy is defeated."

With the note still in his hand, Theo remained silent.

Looking at Theo, a young soldier, the messenger pitied him. "It is not easy–this battle we are called to fight–but it is necessary. I cannot tell you when it will be over. We are unable to know how long it lasts. How can someone know when a battle is over until the end? You fight for as long as you are able, for as long as you have strength, for as long as you have breath. Do not grow weary of well doing. When the King comes, as I know he will, he shall smite the foes, and they will kneel or die before him. Nothing can stand or prevail against the King. We must each decide where we are going to stand. As for me, no matter what happens, I choose to stand and follow my King." Pointing at the note, he asked, "What will *you* choose?"

Theo stared at the note. He knew the messenger was right. The battle would not simply go away, and to live under the rule of the King of the Lowlands was not an option. The words of the messenger replayed in his mind, *"The enemy is a liar. If you live by his terms, you will not live but surely die."* It was time for him to make his stand. It was time for him to fight.

Crumbling the threat, he threw it to the wind and straightened his shoulders. A peace settled over him as he took his stand. Picking up his sword, he stood beside the messenger. "This is the path I choose."

The sun rose above the horizon, and the two stood ready to fight.

---

You may wonder what happens next. Is the enemy defeated? Do they live? Does the King of the Highlands come?

He does, and in the end, the enemy is defeated.

However, whether the messenger and Theo lived past the battle or died in it is not important. The importance lies in what they did while they lived, what they did when faced with the battles.

We all have a choice. Some dream of a peaceful ceasefire. Some abandon the post and attempt to flee. Some surrender to the temptation and lies of the enemy. Some stand and fight.

God has a purpose for each one of us. He equips us for a spiritual battle against our spiritual enemy. He does not want us to be ignorant of the devil's schemes. He strengthens us for what lies ahead, but we must choose what side to stand on and what path to take. Life is not about the pleasure and treasure we get out of it. Life is about God's truth, His righteousness, peace, faith, salvation, and Spirit. It is about being a soldier of Christ.

# We are Chosen

Theo's stand reflects the spiritual fight we will encounter as Christians. When we choose Christ, we become a new creation, a place for Him to dwell, and we are given the responsibility to care for and protect His temple–our spiritual castle. The King of the Highlands represents Christ and the Father, and Theo represents humanity. Satan, portrayed as the King of the Lowlands, takes note of those who turn from sin to Christ, and it is his aim to take them down. Satan encamps against us. His army surrounds us on all sides, but God has provided spiritual armor for the battles ahead, just like the King equipped Theo with the armory. We do not have to go into battle unprepared. Nevertheless, God grants us freedom to choose. He does not force us to take up arms. We must choose to put on the armor He provides, and we must be familiar with the weapons He has given us. Along with this armor, Christ tells us, "I will never leave you nor forsake you."[1] Just as the King of the Highlands sent a messenger to help Theo, God sends us a Messenger and Helper, the Holy Spirit, who teaches and fights alongside us. We never enter this fight alone, and we should never choose to enter it unarmed.

> Ephesians 6:10-20 states: "10 Finally, my brethren, be strong in the Lord and in the power of His might. 11 Put on the whole armor of God, that you may be able to stand against the wiles of the devil. 12 For we do not wrestle against flesh and blood, but against principalities, against powers, against

the rulers of the darkness of this age, against spiritual hosts of wickedness in the heavenly places. 13 Therefore take up the whole armor of God, that you may be able to withstand in the evil day, and having done all, to stand. 14 Stand therefore, having girded your waist with truth, having put on the breastplate of righteousness, 15 and having shod your feet with the preparation of the gospel of peace; 16 above all, taking the shield of faith with which you will be able to quench all the fiery darts of the wicked one. 17 And take the helmet of salvation, and the sword of the Spirit, which is the word of God; 18 praying always with all prayer and supplication in the Spirit, being watchful to this end with all perseverance and supplication for all the saints–19 and for me, that utterance may be given to me, that I may open my mouth boldly to make known the mystery of the gospel, 20 for which I am an ambassador in chains; that in it I may speak boldly, as I ought to speak."

Chapter six of Ephesians is the armory where we find our spiritual armor. Here the Apostle Paul speaks in a language that reflects a soldier's training. Just as the church in Ephesus was in a spiritual war, so are we. We are called to fight and be warriors for Christ. Our weapons are not carnal. They are not of this world. Our weapons are spiritual and have power to demolish the strongholds of a spiritual enemy.[2] Let us prepare. We must put on our spiritual armor as the messenger put on the armor for Theo, and as the messenger explained each piece of armor, we must explore the purpose each piece holds for us. First, we will address how the battle is real, even if we cannot see it, and how we have been chosen and called by God. Secondly, we will look at being called to fight as Paul rallies us with his words and God's calling for His people. Thirdly, we will address where our strength comes from and the importance of standing firm. Fourthly, we will move into studying the different pieces of armor: the belt of truth, breastplate of righteousness, shoes of the preparation of the gospel of peace, shield of faith, helmet of salvation, and the sword of the Spirit. Once we have studied the armor, we will focus on prayer, consequences, and taking action. I pray that this study will be basic training to teach and equip us for the battles we face.

# -A Real War-

Paul tells us in Ephesians chapter six to put on the armor of God, and he warns us of the enemy who fights against us. The war is real. History proves it. Scripture confirms and authenticates it. Scripture speaks of wars in the heavenlies and of wrestling against spiritual hosts of darkness.[3] Paul is not creating a hypothetical situation. He is explaining the reality of the spiritual war Christians are engaged in. We are in a war, whether we realize it or not. As Christians, we go to church and read the Bible, but we often do not grasp the reality of the spiritual world around us. In fact, we often choose to ignore it because we do not understand, or we do not want to fight. We want life to be easy, blessed, at peace, but ignoring the truth does not change it or make it irrelevant. I can choose not to acknowledge that the sky is blue, but that does not change the fact that the sky is blue. I can choose to ignore that water is wet, but that does not change the fact that it is wet. I can choose to believe that fire is not hot, but that does not change the reality. Revelation says repeatedly, "He who has an ear, let him hear what the Spirit says to the churches."[4] We are in spiritual warfare. However, if we choose to dismiss the truth of the spiritual battle around us, we are putting ourselves in danger and all those who are around us. We are unbelieving. We are exposed. We are weaponless and hopeless. When the enemy comes—and he *will* come—how will we defend ourselves against an enemy we believe, we hope, does not exist? We must wake up and realize the battle is real, and we are called to fight it. We are warriors of light and soldiers in a spiritual fight against the enemy of darkness.

## -A Chosen Soldier-

Theo was chosen by the King of the Highlands, just as we are chosen by God. When Theo made the declaration to follow the King, the King set him apart and gave him the responsibility of a castle. When we choose to follow Christ our King, we are set apart, and while we may not have a literal or physical castle, we have a spiritual one. 1 Corinthians 6:19 says, ". . . your body is the temple of the Holy Spirit. . . ." It is our responsibility to protect and care for our temple, our spiritual castle. We are no longer to be like the rest of the world. We are to be His soldiers and serve Him. We are part of His army. Revelation 17:14 says, "Those who are with Him are called, chosen, and faithful." We are His soldiers, called to fight the good fight.[5] Peter states it in this way, "You are a chosen generation, a royal priesthood, a holy nation, His own special people, that you may proclaim the praises of Him who called you out of darkness into His marvelous light."[6] We are called out of darkness. No longer are we to be part of the evil that goes on in this world. No longer are we to be under the rule of the kingdom of darkness but active warriors in the Lord's army. With that position comes responsibility and commitment. We are called to a higher standard. We are to flee youthful lusts, avoid what is unrighteous, pursue righteousness, holiness, truth, and bear His name.[7] Bearing that name comes with responsibility. We are called to be like Him, to be holy like Christ is holy.[8] But how do we achieve holiness? We must imitate and follow the One who is Holy. Christ is our example, and we are to "follow in His steps."[9] We must lay down our desires and seek first the Kingdom of heaven. We must take up our cross daily–dying to self and walking in obedience to the Father. We are given examples of Christian warriors before us who took up their cross, laid down their lives, and lived for Christ. We are to imitate them; Paul says to follow him as he follows Christ.[10] He tells Timothy to "hold fast the pattern . . .you have heard from me."[11] James, the brother of Jesus Christ, writes to the churches giving them an example of the prophets, those who followed God in obedience.[12] Those are examples within scripture. There are examples of godly Christian solders who followed Christ to death throughout Christian history. Consider the apostles, the martyrs of the early church, and countries of Christians who were hated and destroyed for faithfully following their King. And there are people in our own lives we can look to as examples to follow.

As chosen soldiers, we are called to be responsible, like Theo, to defend and care for what the Lord has given us. God gives each of us things for which we are responsible. In the gospel of Matthew, there is a parable of three servants. In the parable, each servant was given a number of talents. Two of them invested their talents and did something with what they were given. The third servant took his talent, put it in the dirt, and left it until the master's return. However, he knew this would not please his master. Jesus said that the servant believed his master "to be a hard man" and "was afraid, and went and hid [the] talent in the ground."[13] This was not the servant's talent. It was given to him by the master. It belonged to the master. He knew the master would want profit and action, but the servant only thought about what he wanted and did not aim to please his master, rejecting and ignoring the responsibility given him. In consequence, the servant lost what he had and was taken away from the master's presence, cast into darkness. All the servants were chosen by the master, but each servant had a choice to make. The two were faithful and responsible. The third servant was not faithful or responsible. He chose not to honor or even fear his master's wishes and then was dismissed and cast away. We are servants of God, and we need to know what our heavenly Master desires. For us to know what the Master desires, we need to have a relationship with Him. Christ Himself prayed for us to have this relationship that we become one with the Father, just as He and the Father are one.[14] To know the Father we must know the Son. Scripture says no one comes to the Father except through Christ.[15] But it is not enough merely to know about Him, we must know Him on a personal level. The Pharisees intellectually knew *about* the Messiah, but they did not recognize Him when He stood right before them. While encountering them, Christ says, "You search the Scriptures" looking for the Messiah, and yet He tells them, "You have not known [God]."[16] Throughout His teaching, Christ stresses how He and the Father are One and the importance of knowing Him. Jesus encourages the disciples "If you had known Me, you would have known My Father also."[17] When we know the Master, we will know what He desires. He desires our heart, soul, mind, and strength; He emphasizes this when He answers those who ask what the greatest commandment is.[18] He wants our love, and when we love the Master, we obey His commands.[19] When we obey, we are being responsible with our actions. It was Theo's responsibility to guard the castle. He would not have been a good soldier if he had fled and abandoned the castle. Likewise, as followers of Christ, we are to know Christ, know His desires, and never abandon Him or our positions.

## -A Helper-

When Christ calls us, He does not abandon us. He does not step back and say 'good luck.' Never. He walks beside us like the Good Shepherd that He is.[20] He will never leave us.[21] Like the King of the Highlands in the story, He is not far from us, and He sends us His Helper. In John 14:26, Christ tells the disciples that the Father will send the Holy Spirit as a Helper, a Counselor. This promise was not just for the early disciples, but it is for all Jesus' disciples, then and now. We are to listen to the Holy Spirit when He impresses upon us or speaks to us. He will teach us and remind us of Christ.[22] He will direct us in how to use the armor God has provided. If we will listen and obey, He will guide us in the way of the Lord.[23] But if we ignore the Messenger and block our ears, we will be like the fool in Proverbs who Wisdom laughs at because his downfall is coming.[24] Can you imagine what could have happened had Theo not listened to the messenger? If he had ignored the call, he would have been there helpless and with nothing to defend himself. When the enemy broke through, he would have been like a twig blown in the wind with no defense or protection, snapped in half. The enemy would have destroyed him. But the King of the Highlands did not abandon him, and Theo listened to the messenger's warnings. He prepared for the battle, put on his armor, and fought, taking a stand against the enemy. We need to do the same. God has given us what we need to fight the battles before us. Now, we must decide—will we stand firm in Him, listen to His call, and follow His directions through the preparation and battles ahead, or will we walk away?

# Be Strong

*"Finally, my brethren, be strong in the Lord and in the power of His might."*
*- Ephesians 6:10*

The messenger tells Theo continually throughout the story to stand strong. Paul encourages Christian believers to "be strong in the Lord." Our physical strength cannot overcome the spiritual war we wage. We cannot hold our own against an enemy who knows all the arts and ways of war, but with the Lord's help we can stand. Theo needed the armor and the messenger's guidance to help him stand against the enemy. Our strength does not come from us; it comes from the One who is greater. Nothing is too great for God, because with God all things are possible.[1] He enables us to bend a bow of bronze.[2] He instructs us in the way to go.[3] Because the Lord is our strength and arms us for battle, the enemy shall be subdued under us.[4] As Paul proclaims, if God is for me, nothing can stand against me.[5] This does not mean that nothing will come against me, but that **when** the enemy comes, he will not be able to stand. In the story, the enemy did not leave Theo alone just because he inherited a castle. In fact, the enemy increased his oppression and waged war against him. Nevertheless, Theo stood firm. At the end, the enemy will fall or flee. Scripture says to "submit to God. Resist the devil and he will flee from you."[6] First, we submit to God. Next, we resist the devil. *Then* he leaves. However, this is often a longer process than we realize. We must first learn to submit to God, and then the rest follows. We are God's children, chosen by Him. We are His handpicked soldiers. Nevertheless, before a soldier is sent to battle, he or she must learn to submit to and obey the commander, just like Theo had to learn to use his armor and listen to the messenger's instruction. If we are to endure and fight the spiritual battles that come, we must learn to obey and follow God, for we stand strong in Him and not in ourselves.

## -Joy that Strengthens-

What does that strength look like? For Theo, the first layer of protection he wore was the chain mail, which represented joy. The messenger explained it is like padding between you and the outside. Joy is a protection factor. Nehemiah says, "The joy of the Lord is your strength."[7] David says, "The Lord is the strength of my life; of whom shall I be afraid?"[8] God gives us His joy, and His joy strengthens our inner being. Without joy, when the enemy strikes, we are easily devastated, but if we have the joy of the Lord, we are not easily torn down. Because we know that God's joy strengthens us, we can rise without fear and face our enemy with strength beyond ourselves, a strength he does not know. While in a battle, we may not feel joyful because the joy comes not from the battle but from what lies afterward. It is found in the victory of walking in obedience to the Father. When Christ faced the battle of the cross, scripture says, "for the joy that was set before Him [He] endured the cross."[9] It was not for the joy of the cross, but for the joy of what was to come *after* the cross. Crucifixion is not a joyful experience. It is a tortuous way to die. In fact, it was the worst death sentence of that time. Christ's joy was not in the agony of being nailed to a cross but in what came after the trial and suffering. He knew victory was coming—the joy of the resurrection and ascension to the throne of God, the joy of obedience to the Father, and the joy of being with the Father. Now we, too, can have joy in Him because Christ defeated sin and the grave by rising from the dead and opening the door for us to enter heaven. While joy amidst the battle may seem impossible, with God nothing is impossible.[10]

We know that in this world there will be trials, but we also know that Christ has overcome the world.[11] His eternal mindset of victorious joy aids us. But do not be deceived, the enemy will try to convince us to lay aside the protection of Christ's joy and walk in fear. Yet remember, like the messenger told Theo, and scripture confirms, we are not given a spirit of fear but of power, love, and a sound mind.[12] The enemy tries to weaken our strength by stealing our joy and filling our minds with fear. If he can replace our garment of joy with a cloak of fear, our first defense against the enemy is gone. Fear causes us to bleed out, but joy heals and strengthens. Our protection, our joy, comes when we give our fears and worries over to Christ and trust Him to get us through the fight—*all* the way through. The strength we need for this war does not come from ourselves but from God. And the joy He strengthens us with does not come from the things He gives us but from Himself. Therefore, even if we were to lose everything, we could be like Job and still rejoice and say, "Blessed be the name of the Lord."[13] The King of the Highlands is coming. Our victorious joy may not be in the here and now, but Christ will win the victory in the end, and it is with Him that we stand and rejoice.

## -Our Focus-

Furthermore, to be strong in the Lord, our focus must be properly set. We need to be focused for battle. We, as soldiers in Christ's army, all have a responsibility to stand for Him, in His strength and power against principalities, powers, rulers of the darkness, and spiritual hosts of wickedness. We cannot enter this battle focused on our own strength. Like Theo in the story, when we look to ourselves for deliverance, our strength will fail. The simple truth is, like Theo, we are not strong enough, but God *is*. Do not be worried and consumed with thinking how great the enemy is or how outnumbered and alone you feel. When Theo focused on the number of the enemy, he grew fearful and lost his shield. Those thoughts place the focus on ourselves and weaken us in the fight. If we are not looking at and listening to Christ, we are looking elsewhere and listening to something else, and we will lose. Where is your focus? The focus must not be on ourselves or on anything else but on God. Paul tells Timothy, "No one engaged in warfare entangles himself with the affairs of this life, that he may please him who enlisted him as a soldier."[14] Choosing to focus on God is a constant battle. Nevertheless, we must remember why we are here on this earth. It is not about us. We are like Theo, a soldier here to do the King's will and protect His castle. We are here to do the will of God, and as Jesus so clearly put it–in the greatest commandment–, we are to "love the Lord [our] God with all [our] heart, with all [our] soul, with all [our] mind, and with all [our] strength."[15] If we are loving God with everything we have, then that is where our focus will be. That is where our joy and hope will originate. The book of Proverbs says, "Trust in the Lord with all your heart, and lean not on your own understanding."[16] Focus on the Lord; trust Him with everything. He has this. God is going to take the enemy down. Focus on God, and He will use us as His instruments and soldiers. In His strength, we enter the fight. In His strength, we stand and face the enemy. In His strength, we win the victory.

# Wiles of the Devil

*"Put on the whole armor of God, that you may be able to stand against the wiles of the devil. For we do not wrestle against flesh and blood, but against principalities, against powers, against the rulers of the darkness of this age, against spiritual hosts of wickedness in the heavenly places."*
*- Ephesians 6:11-12*

In the story, the messenger gives Theo insight concerning the enemy he faces. Ephesians 6:11-12 give us insight on the enemy. Paul cautions us that we are to "stand against the wiles of the devil." Wiles are interpreted as tricks, traps, and deceitful cunnings. Like the enemy in the story who pretended to be a helpless beggar to gain entrance, the devil lays traps before us. From the beginning of creation, he has been deceiving souls. In the Garden of Eden, Satan deceived and tricked Eve into eating of the fruit of the tree of the knowledge of good and evil.[1] God warned Eve's son, Cain, that sin crouched at his door waiting to catch him, and it did.[2] The devil waits for opportunities to sneak in and destroy us, but we do not have to be ignorant of his schemes. Paul warns the Christians in Corinth lest, Satan should take advantage of them, that "we are not ignorant of his devices."[3] We know who the enemy is, and we know his wiles. As the messenger helped Theo to see the ruse and deception of the enemy, God shows us the truth about the devil and warns us of his wiles.

## -Scriptural Examples-

Flip through the scriptures and you will see how the devil uses his wiles to deceive people and how often he succeeds. So be aware: the enemy is not retreating from the battlefield. He employs fear to distract us from trusting God. The Israelite people were distracted with fear when they saw the armies of Egypt. They were afraid for their lives. They were cut off by the Red Sea and pursued by Pharaoh's armies. They had just witnessed the power of God in Egypt, but they were caught in fear.[4] Joseph's brothers were distracted with envy and hate and sold their own brother into slavery.[5] Moses tried to act in his own strength and save the people of Israel before it was God's timing.[6] Joshua was distracted by the appearance of the Gibeonites when they lied about who they were; he did not ask God before he made promises that he should not have made.[7] Samson's desire for Delilah led to his capture, loss of eyesight, and eventual death.[8] David did not flee the temptation of lust for Bathsheba, and because of his actions, blood and war never left his house, *and* he lost his child.[9] Solomon was the wisest man that ever lived, but his heart was distracted from God because of his love of women. Eventually, Solomon went after the gods of his foreign wives and forsook God's covenant.[10] Jeroboam was distracted by jealousy. He did not trust God but built two golden calves which distracted the people and led them astray. Consequently, God took the kingdom from his family.[11] Gehazi, the servant of Elisha, fell to the temptation of worldly pleasures when he sought the reward from Naaman. His consequence was leprosy on him and his family.[12] Jonah was God's prophet, but he gave into the temptation to flee from God's command to prophesy to the people of Nineveh.[13]

In the New Testament, the devil's devices are also seen. The priests and elders, who were the teachers of the law, were tempted and overwhelmed with envy and plotted to kill Christ.[14] Confusion over Christ's statement regarding his body and blood (the Eucharist) caused many to turn away.[15] Pilate wanted to release Jesus but was trapped by public opinion.[16] Even Peter, one of Christ's disciples, was tempted with fear to lie. Being distracted by the fear of discovery, arrest, and execution, he denied Christ three times.[17] Demas was deceived by his love of the world and left the truth.[18] Ananias and Sapphira lied for self-glory.[19] These are just some examples of people in scripture who were tempted, tricked, or deceived by the enemy and gave into his distractions.

# -Hidden Temptations-

We may think, "How could they do such a thing?" or "I would never do *that*." Remember the stories the messenger told. The temptations are not always obvious. Not all the enemy's temptations are clear traps. Some may even appear like a good choice. The man who fought for his family did not consider the terms of the enemy as a trap leading to death. He wanted to save his family. The enemy deceived him into thinking surrender was his only way to save them, yet in the end they all lost. Some of the temptations are even subtler to perceive. They appear more like the beggar at the gate: they have the appearance of one thing, but in truth they are cloaked with deception and are detrimental.

A radio preacher once spoke about how Satan will entice us with the 'best' of evil–things that the world may see as good but are deceitful. For example, the devil employs something that appears good, but his aim is for us to sin. He wants us to listen to him and not the Father. He wants us to trust him and turn our eyes away from God. Think of Eve and the fruit–it appeared good, but the consequence was death.[20]

Another example is the children of Israel. Believing the ten spies over the two, they refused to enter the promised land. They were rebuked, then they decided they would act and take the land after God said to go to the desert. They were defeated.[21] They thought they knew what was best.

King Saul was given a mission to destroy the Amalekites. However, he saved the best of his enemy's goods, claiming it as a sacrifice for God, yet God had said to destroy *everything*.[22]

These choices may have appeared as good, honoring decisions, but they were not done in obedience to God. The devil had deceived them using the temptation to fulfill their own desires, rather than to obey, but obedience is better than a sacrifice, and to heed God is better than giving a gift.[23]

# -Rejoin the Fight-

Some people fell before the enemy and did not rise again. Others fell, repented, and got up again. Did God still use these individuals for His glory? Yes, but they had to choose to rejoin the fight and stand against the enemy. Just like Theo, after he fell, he got back up and kept fighting. They, too, had to choose to put their focus back on God, get up, and go again. Joshua, who acted without God's guidance, sought God's direction the next time and obeyed.[24] Samson, though physically blinded by the enemy, stood back up to finish the fight.[25] David, who had done wrong with Bathsheba, repented and refocused his mind and actions on God.[26] Peter repented, wept over his denial, and got up to fight the good fight.[27]

God wants us to get back up if we have fallen; He wants us to fight again. In First Samuel chapter twelve, when the people had sinned by asking for a king, Samuel tells them, "Do not fear. You have done all this wickedness; yet do not turn aside from following the Lord, but serve the Lord with all your heart. And do not turn aside; for then you would go after empty things which cannot profit or deliver, for they are nothing. For the Lord will not forsake His people."[28]

There is hope for us. If we fall, we can get back up in God's mercy and strength. No matter what temptation you may have fallen prey to, if we do as Samuel said and turn from our iniquity and serve the Lord with all our heart, then He will not forsake us. Where have you fallen? God knows the trials and temptations we face. He is aware of the wiles the devil uses, and He provides us with the weapons to fight and the path to take. Paul assures us that God will provide a way out of the temptations and enable us to bear it.[29] Even though the devil will shoot fiery arrows at us and use temptations, distractions, and traps to stop us from following Christ, his temptations need not be fatal or even debilitating. We must hold onto God and fight to the death against the deceiver. Be aware of the enemy's wiles; do not let him succeed. Press on until the war is ended.

# Physical and Spiritual Battles

*"For we do not wrestle against flesh and blood, but against principalities, against powers, against the rulers of the darkness of this age, against spiritual hosts of wickedness in the heavenly places." - Ephesians 6:12*

In the story, The messenger cautions Theo that while he is physically armored for the battle, he must also fight the battle in his mind and not let the enemy gain a foothold in his thoughts. In Ephesians, Paul references two types of battle: the physical (the "flesh and blood") and the spiritual (the "principalities"). However, he warns us that the real battle lies not against the physical but against the spiritual enemy. The enemy has many allies: sin nature, the world, pride, anger, malice, and the list goes on. He will use or ally himself with anything he can to keep us from the fight. One powerful ally of the enemy we all encounter is our own sin nature, and within that sin nature, our fleshly carnal mindset, lies iniquity. Iniquity is aligning yourself with your own will and not that of God's. We should not be surprised by this ally because according to scripture, our flesh fights against our spirit.[1] Theo had his own inner struggle–would he continue to fight, or would he flee? His flesh, the human desire, wanted to leave it all behind, but his spirit knew the truth. He needed to fight. There is a war between the physical and the spiritual. Satan sets up stumbling blocks, but some of the pitfalls are of our own making, and he will take advantage of every situation he can. The enemy took advantage of the man in the story who wanted riches. He used the carnal desire and allied himself with that and destroyed the man. When our humanity, our flesh, is fighting our spirit, we must understand that we are being attacked on the spiritual level while being distracted with the physical. In these situations, we must fight two opponents: we must fight our fleshly desires, and we must fight Satan's attacks. The man who wanted riches did not fight the flesh, and he lost his life. The flesh is loud and will lash out at us demanding we appease it. We must learn to fight the fleshly desires and listen to the voice of God in our lives. A soldier hears many voices on the battlefield, and he must choose which commands to follow. The voices claiming our attention and filling our ears are those of others, the enemy, God, and ourselves. Every voice vies for our attention, but only one voice matters on this battlefield, and that is God's. We must learn to focus on God's voice and listen for the Holy Spirit's warnings and calls.

## -Choosing a Voice-

Choosing what voice to focus on is a battle of its own, and we must win it in our minds. Have you ever talked yourself into or out of something? We can focus so much on one voice that we ignore and drown out all others. If we focus on ourselves, we often miss when God's quiet voice speaks to us. We must enact self-control and fight to stay focused on Christ and the battles before us. In the story, Theo heard the direction from the messenger, he heard the shouts of the coming foes, and he heard his own worry and doubt. He had to choose what voice he was going to listen to. If we do not choose well, those voices which are the loudest, or pushiest, will take control of our thoughts, and those are most often not of God. In scripture, the prophet Elijah had to learn that the Lord's voice was still, like a small wind, like a whisper.[2] In John, chapter three, Jesus describes the Spirit in this manner as a "wind [that] blows where it wishes, and you hear the sound of it, but cannot tell where it comes from and where it goes. So is everyone who is born of the Spirit."[3] Those who are not of the Lord's army cannot tell where or when the Holy Spirit moves and directs the soldiers of God, but we, as His soldiers, know the Father through the Son, and by the Father we are given the Holy Spirit. It is He who leads us in battle, yet we must listen for His voice as one listens for a soft wind. Constantly, scripture reflects how the Lord allows us the freedom to choose, which also means that He does not force us to follow His voice but lets us decide who or what we listen to. Therefore, we must learn to home in on God's voice and His words, fill ourselves with scripture so we know what aligns with His word and what does not. We can easily become weary of all the different shouts of the enemy, and we just want to give in because we are tired, but we cannot surrender our minds to the enemy. Do not let yourself stop fighting, even if you are tired. Conquer the body. Ask the Lord for strength. Keep going. Even if you do not feel like you have the strength, take one day, one moment, and one breath at a time. In the story, Theo continued to shoot arrows from the watchtower, even when his arms grew tired. His flesh rebelled and wanted to stop, but he knew he had to continue. He told himself "No" and kept fighting. We must tell our flesh "No" when it wants to focus our attention off spiritual battles and onto the things of the world. The man who wanted the riches should have fought his fleshly desire for wealth. Instead, he gave in, listening to the voice of the enemy. Theo had the mental battle of choosing between surrendering to the enemy's terms or fighting to the death. He had to choose if he was going to follow his own self-preservation, or if he was going to say "No" and choose the desires, the will, of the King–to stand and fight. We, too, have the mental battles of choosing our will or that of the Father's. If I choose my own will and focus on my own desires, I will not be ready for the attacks of the enemy. I will be consumed with my own thoughts, and I will be deterred from the battle. We must fight against the fleshly desire and take our thoughts captive, as Paul tells the church at Corinth, "to the obedience of Christ."[4] And what does that look like? It looks like surrender to the Father. Christ's obedience was total surrender to the Father. As He said in the garden, "not My will, but Yours, be done."[5] It is saying "No" to what we want and seeking what God wants, humbling ourselves before Him and being obedient to His will.

## -Conquering the Flesh-

To win the battle against ourselves, it is necessary to fight and train our flesh. We must put ourselves into submission under Christ and under the Father. Our flesh, our sin nature, desires carnal things and not the things of God. However, our spirit desires things of the Spirit, things above.[6] If built up, exercised, and trained, our spirit can and will win over the flesh. On the other hand, if we let our flesh have its way and silence the Spirit, we will surrender to our sin nature and lose the spiritual battle. When Theo was supposed to be on watch, he gave into the desire of the flesh to sleep. He did not fight the battle against the flesh, and he nearly died. The small battles we wage with the flesh may not seem like much, but do not be deceived, they are the beginning of a greater fight. For if we cannot control our own bodies physically, how can we control ourselves in a spiritual fight? The more we practice fighting our fleshly desires, the stronger our spirit grows. The more we learn to say "No" to ourselves and "Yes" to God, the better soldiers we become. In First Corinthians chapter nine, Paul talks about having to train and discipline our bodies for the spiritual battle ahead.[7] Our physical trials are a practice ground for us. Once we learn to fight and conquer our flesh, we are prepared to encounter stronger spiritual fights. Scripture says, "to whom much is given, from him much will be required."[8] God gives us little battles to practice, learn from, and conquer. Then He gives us bigger battles. Theo began his training with very little knowledge or skill. Yet, as he practiced with the messenger, he learned more and grew stronger. He fought from the tower and then face-to-face with the enemy. As soldiers, we must make a conscientious act to fight the small practice battles so we will be prepared to fight the greater spiritual battles. In a similar manner, the soldiers and competitors in Roman games and races had to first practice and pass the preliminary smaller rounds before they could even compete, advance, or receive a victor's crown. This is also the case in the spiritual battles we encounter. If we want to win the victory, we must first conquer the smaller carnal battles within ourselves. But remember, if we keep our eyes on the things of this world, the things of the flesh, and refuse to acknowledge the spiritual war, we wound ourselves and lose sight of what is really happening. The battle with the flesh is indeed a battle in the spirit. If we realize that, we can pray and be watchful against this scheme of the devil and his desire to draw our thoughts away from God and the heavenly.

## -Physical Versus Spiritual-

We must be cautious. There are times when the physical battles we face will intensify and, if we are not careful, will overwhelm us. We must not lose focus. The urgency or pain of some physical battles draws and demands attention, yet when we focus on the flesh we are distracted from the spiritual war. In this world, we struggle with death, sicknesses, heartache, and pain, but we must not let the world's demands hinder us from the spiritual fight. When Theo saw the enemy camped around the castle, his focus was on the urgency of the situation. He saw his need for rescue, but did not realize his need to fight until the messenger showed him. We see the physical, but at times we do not recognize the spiritual. There is always a spiritual battle going on. In the physical, we will reach this point of exhaustion in ourselves. Here we must stop and pray. Psalm 121:1-2 says, "I will lift up my eyes to the hills–from whence comes my help? My help comes from the Lord, who made heaven and earth." Ask God what is truly going on. Ask what the spiritual battle is. Ask Him to open your eyes. Ask Him to strengthen you. Some of the physical trials we encounter are to grow our faith, and then there are the physical trials that are reflections of the spiritual battles above. When Jesus taught His disciples about praying, He spoke the phrase, "on earth as it is in heaven."[9] What occurs in the spirit world is often reflected in the physical. In the book of Daniel, Daniel had been praying and fasting, searching for God to reveal an answer to his dream. Daniel was greatly troubled within himself, yet he had set his focus on God, to search out truth. He prayed for three weeks and was very weak. In the book of Daniel, chapter ten, a messenger, an angel, comes and speaks to Daniel, telling him, "Do not fear, Daniel, for from the first day that you set your heart to understand, and to humble yourself before your God, your words were heard; and I have come because of your words."[10] Notice how the answer did not reach Daniel right away. Although the angel had been dispatched, the Prince of Persia, not a physical prince but a spiritual enemy and prince of the air, delayed the messenger. He had been fighting with the enemy for three weeks before the angel Michael came to fight alongside him, to relieve him, and then he was able to deliver his message. After the messenger delivered clarity to Daniel, he would return to fight beside Michael.[11] Even with the answer coming to Daniel, he was still exhausted. Daniel tells the angel, "My sorrows have overwhelmed me, and I have retained no strength."[12] Then "the one having the likeness of a man touched [him] and strengthened [him]" saying, "Fear not! Peace be to you; be strong, yes, be strong!" and Daniel was strengthened.[13] Not only did the Lord give clarity to Daniel, but He strengthened him for what lay ahead. The spiritual battle and struggle between the heavenly hosts was reflected in the physical struggle Daniel endured. We constantly struggle in the physical. When these struggles occur, we need to look to God and pray. There is likely something going on spiritually that we do not know. Another example comes from Second Kings. There was a Shunamite woman who was barren. The man of God prayed for her, and God blessed her with a child. One day, the boy became sick and died. When the Shunamite woman came to the man of God and cried, the servant came to push her away, but Elisha said, "Let her alone; for her soul is in deep distress, and the Lord has hidden it from me, and has not told me."[14] Elisha did not know what had taken place, that her son had died, but he knew something was behind her agony. We, too, do not know all that takes place unless God gives us eyes to see. In Second Kings chapter six, Elisha and his servant are surrounded by the army of Syria. The servant cries out, "What shall we do?" and Elisha answers, "Do not fear, for those who are with us are more than those who are with them."[15] Elisha prayed that the servant's eyes would be opened, and "the Lord opened the eyes of the young man, and he saw. And behold, the mountain was full of horses and chariots of fire all around Elisha."[16] There is a spiritual battle raging, but we can only see it if we humble ourselves and let God open our eyes. However, He gives us the choice. We can see, or we can shut our eyes and ignore the battle. Yet, what happens if we close our eyes and sleep?

## -Do Not Slumber-

The book of Proverbs warns us against being a sluggard. In chapter six, Solomon says, "How long will you slumber, O sluggard? When will you rise from your sleep?"[17] He warns that if we do nothing, if we continue to slumber, "poverty will come upon [us] like a prowler, and [our] need like an armed man."[18] Our enemy is ready and armed, and if he can deceive us into thinking that nothing is going on and keep us "asleep," he will destroy us. Paul writes in his letter to the Romans that the hour has come "to awake out of sleep; for now our salvation is nearer than when we first believed. The night is far spent, the day is at hand. Therefore let us cast off the works of darkness, and let us put on the armor of light."[19] We must be alert and stay awake so the enemy does not choke us like Theo was choked when he fell asleep. Yet, if we choose to ignore the supernatural fighting around us, we are spiritually asleep.

# -A Light-

Paul tells us now is the time to act. Wake up and put on your armor so you can cast off darkness, a spiritual darkness that Peter proclaims we have been called out of.[20] Darkness consumes and brings death, but light shines and brings life. As Christ is the light of the world, He brings life, and He calls us to have the light of life.[21] In his letter to the Ephesians, Paul tells us we are to be children of the light.[22] We are to be like a city on a hill that gives light to all around.[23] But be forewarned: when a light shines in the darkness, all see it–friends and foes. Those come who desire the light for good, and others come who desire to fight against it and put it out. Our allies will embrace and protect the light. The enemy will attempt to snuff out the light, and there will be a fight. Scripture confirms that the darkness hates the light and fights against it.[24] We must stand our ground as a city of light, because when a light is covered and does not receive oxygen, it suffocates. Satan wants to suffocate our spirits, and if we do nothing and ignore the spiritual battles, he may succeed. As Christians, we are called to put on armor of light and "fight the good fight,"[25] to wrestle against "principalities, against powers, against rulers of the darkness."[26]

We need our armor on us always, so when an enemy comes upon us suddenly, we are protected and strengthened to withstand the attack. He is not going to wait, and we should not wait for an attack before we suit up. If we wait, we will make ourselves vulnerable to the arrows of the enemy. We will be targets without protection. It will be our own fault if we are hit. It is our choice to put on the armor and protection God has provided, or our choice not to put it on. Before the messenger came, Theo was standing unprotected. He knew there was an armory, but it was not until the messenger arrived that Theo put on the protection provided. Have you put on the armor of God? God would not give us His armor if He did not intend for us to wear it. Paul says to "put on" the armor of God. That is an order. Dress for battle now. The Lord does not want any to perish.[27] He has given us the ability to survive and gain victory in this spiritual fight by providing us with armor of light and weapons to fight. The question is: Will you stand with Him and fight?

# Standing Ready

*"Therefore take up the whole armor of God, that you may be able to withstand in the evil day, and having done all, to stand. Stand therefore, having girded your waist with truth, having put on the breastplate of righteousness, and having shod your feet with the preparation of the gospel of peace; above all, taking the shield of faith with which you will be able to quench all the fiery darts of the wicked one. And take the helmet of salvation, and the sword of the Spirit, which is the word of God." - Ephesians 6:13-17*

We are entering a battle zone. As the messenger prepared Theo for battle, we, too, are required to prepare. Verses thirteen through seventeen describe the necessities required for what lies ahead and give instructions on what is needed to stand with Christ. Verse fourteen begins with the word "stand." We must predetermine that we will stand up and fight. We must mentally and spiritually *choose* to stand firm in our decision to stand with Christ.

Fighting the enemy is not an easy task, and at different times you will be required to fight differently. Sometimes we are called to fight hand-to-hand combat. Other times, we are called to be the archers. We could be called to fight on the frontlines at the charge or told to help the fight by standing our ground. The latter has different challenges than charging at the front. Standing our ground takes time and patience. It takes dedication and determination. It takes faithfulness, self-control, and discipline. It takes a mindset. Not to say the other does not, but from what I've experienced, it is exercised differently, especially through patience and dedication. Before going into battle, a soldier must make the mental decision of whether he or she is willing to fight and, if necessary, die. We, too, must make the decision, just like Theo had to make his decision. Are we truly willing to fight for Christ? Are we willing to die for Him? Are we willing, like Paul, to put to death our human passions that war against our spirit?[1] How can we effectively war against other enemies if we are in constant war within ourselves?

## -Predetermine Your Stance-

The spiritual battle is always transpiring. If we do not decide in advance where and with whom we stand, the enemy will deceive, tempt, trick, and cause us to lose our focus. His goal is to take us down with him. Satan is not giving up. He never stops attacking. He does not get tired of tempting, torturing, and tormenting Christ's followers. He knows, and scripture tells us, his time is limited.[2] Therefore, he is determined to take us down, and we need to be more determined to stand. If he can get us to lose focus, he will have the upper hand and our minds will no longer be on the battle or on its importance but caught up in our surroundings or ourselves. Thoughts, like what are we giving up, or what are we missing out on, take captive many soldiers. When temptations or distractions come, we must fight them and stay engaged. If we are distracted from the battle, we must regain our focus. We must keep fighting. We are to take every thought captive to the obedience of Christ.[3] To do this, we ask ourselves, "Is this thought from Christ?" If the answer is "No," we must mentally envision putting it in chains and handing it over to God. He will deal with it. If we do not put everything under the obedience of Christ, the enemy has won a fight within our mind and taken precious ground. This is a fight to the death of the thoughts. We do not want to give any extra power to the enemy! We must stand!

## -The Action of Standing-

But what does it mean to stand? What does that entail? While some may think that standing means doing nothing, it is in fact an action. One of our problems is we often become bored or discontented when we are told to stand still. Many of us want to be doing something, and we feel like we are not doing anything when standing still. However, do not be deceived. We *are* doing something; we are preparing for a fight. We are being obedient, and in obedience we show our love for Christ. He tells the disciples in John 14:15, "If you love Me, keep My commands." It is crucial as a soldier that we obey whatever our Commanding Officer tells us, and when we are told to stand, that is what we need to do. Just as the messenger told Theo to stand firm as the enemy advanced, we, too, are to stand firm in this battle against principalities.

Standing may be one of the hardest actions to execute, yet it is vital in training for battle. Standing is the first step to fighting the enemy. Do not get discouraged. Before soldiers go to battle, they must be prepared to fight–physically with their armor and mentally in their minds. When fighting with any sort of techniques, you must first learn how to stand, how to keep proper balance. If you do not have a good form or stance, the enemy will be able to come in and easily knock you over. You could fall when attempting an attack simply because your feet are not firmly in place. Standing your ground is the first part of fighting the war. To learn how to stand, we must be still. Scripture says, "Be still, and know that I am God."[4] Our first job as a soldier of Christ is to be still. In this practice, we learn to stand, listen to our Commander, and hear His voice. This concept of standing is parallel to waiting. It can be trying. It takes patience and strength. Not many of us are good at it, but sometimes that is simply what is required of us, and through that God wants to strengthen us. Standing still often comes with three human responses that we must conquer–discontentment with what we have been given or told to do, lack of self-discipline, and fear of what is coming.

## -Discontentment-

The first concept of discontentment is very dangerous. It causes us to ignore the Holy Spirit within and focus on the outer man. Often, we end up rushing into situations or fights we were never prepared for or directed to partake in. Maybe we are focused too much on the physical. Maybe we are overzealous for action. Whatever the reason, we must be content with our orders and be obedient. As Paul says, let us be content in whatever state, or with whatever orders we have been given.[5] Discontentment can also lead us to second-guessing our Commanding Officer, Jesus Christ. We know there is a battle raging, and we want to help. However, we can fall into discontentment with our position and start to think we know better than He does (which is most certainly *not* true). While our desire for action can be good, if we have been told to stand still, then this drive for action is detrimental and often deadly. Not only will we hurt ourselves, but we often harm our fellow soldiers, too. For example, let us say you have been placed in charge of a group of ten men. Your orders are to wait until you receive the signal to attack. Hours pass; you are tired of waiting. You reason within yourself that you are needed, or perhaps they forgot to give the signal. You lead the charge. Your men follow. Unknown to you, enemy troops were just deployed to spring an attack from behind. Had you remained in your position, you would have been able to see them and defeat them. Unfortunately, you rushed in too early. Now they are at your heels and attacking your men from the back. Not only are you not able to come to the aid of your comrades, but you are caught unaware in a battle that could have been quickly overcome. In the end, the losses are great. We may not feel like we are doing anything, but standing in obedience to Christ is acting. Once we are ready and standing with God (having surrendered to

God's will), He often sends us out to fight. Theo also was told to "stand strong." He was not told to charge, but to be ready. The time would come when he would fight. And the time did come. The enemy came, and he fought, but it was at the right time. Had he decided to rush forward and meet the enemy outside the wall, he would have been overpowered and killed. And the castle would have been left defenseless. Examples such as these can show the consequences of our actions if we jump into the fight too early and the importance of standing in obedience when we have been told to stand and wait.

## -Self-discipline-

The second concept is a lack of self-discipline. Lack of self-discipline is a dangerous attribute for a soldier. Self-discipline, or self-control, is a vital part of standing. However, if we ignore the training opportunities of learning self-control, we will not be disciplined enough to hold still and wait. Have you ever seen a child who, after being told to stand still, immediately starts walking around or spinning in circles until they fall over? They have very little, if any, self-discipline. They lack any motivation to be still. They do not realize the importance of it. Theo realized the importance of self-discipline as he trained with the messenger. The messenger reminded him how in the middle of war it is not time to focus on our own desires but to be self-disciplined and focus on the battle before us. In his directions, he reminded Theo to stand ready and wait. In war, self-discipline is crucial. It is how a soldier makes himself follow orders. It is how he forces himself to wait. It is how he readies himself to fight. Paul tells the church at Corinth, "I discipline my body and bring it into subjection."[6] Learning to discipline ourselves and say, "No" to the flesh trains and prepares us for the fight and for standing still while we wait. It is a battle within ourselves to maintain patience. We may not be able to control what the enemy brings against us, but we can control ourselves.

We can be self-disciplined. We *must* be self-disciplined so we can remain standing against all odds.

## -Fear-

The third concept–fear–is also dangerous. Fear is defined as a feeling or condition of lacking courage and the mental determination to challenge an enemy or problem. Battles are scary. We realize how small and insignificant we are. We become overwhelmed. When we stand still, we can see the enemy before us. We can hear the battle raging, and we can feel the ground shake. Our minds go crazy with the unknown, of what might happen. We imagine the worst possible outcomes. Too often we get caught up in the scene before us, like Theo when he saw the numerous foes. We either want to run in and fight, when it's not our time, or we want to run and hide. But here Paul says we are called to stand. God has this under control, even if we cannot see how. He knows what is going on. He knows our worries, but we do not need to worry. Scripture says, "Do not worry about tomorrow. . . sufficient for the day is its own trouble."[7] In Matthew 6, Christ tells the people not to worry about what they will eat or drink, for your heavenly Father will care for you.[8] He does care for us both physically and spiritually. Just like with Theo, He provides what we need to face the battle ahead. We must not collapse under fear. He gives us the armor so that we can withstand the enemy right where we are. And like the messenger told Theo, "We are fully equipped to take them on. Do not be afraid." Scripture is full of phrases like "do not be afraid," "do not fear," and "fear not."[9] Peter says, "Do not be afraid of their threats, nor be troubled," and "even if you should suffer for righteousness' sake, you are blessed."[10] We do not need to fear. We need to stand where Christ directs. In His timing, He will let us know when we are to move. We must wait on and trust Him. Our trust in Christ will help us conquer the fear that rises within us. We are not called to fight every battle. Sometimes we are called to stand and be ready to fight, "and having done all, to stand" as Ephesians 6:13 states. Had Theo succumbed to the emotion of fear, he would have fled the battle or surrendered to the demands of the enemy. However, because he did not focus on fear but listened to his commander and stood ready, he was able to fight and prevail when the enemy came.

# -To Stand-

Within Ephesians 6:13-17, Paul uses the words "stand" and "withstand."[11] Both words cover the same action. To withstand is simply a form of standing. It is defined as resisting or standing in opposition. To stand is to hold out against something, remaining firm in endurance or opposition. The action of standing holds enormous meaning. Think about what standing can represent. What is portrayed through the posture of standing? What message do we send when we stand? Standing gives the message and appearance of being unafraid, secure, alert, aware, strong, capable, determined, unmovable, dedicated, ready, waiting, bold, and prepared. That list of characteristics is the message we convey when we stand. This posture of standing not only strengthens us in our resolve of what we must do, but it also represents the power of a soldier of Christ, and that frightens our enemies and lets them know we are ready for war.

Know that when we stand firm we will be noticed by the enemy. He will come against us, and this is not a onetime gig. Just like in Theo's story, the enemy continues to come. And the enemy will continue to fight against us for as long as we keep standing. But do not think that if you surrender to the foe, he will leave you alone or have mercy. Remember the stories the messenger told of how the enemy tricked and deceived the two men. His goal is to kill, steal, and destroy.[12] Do not believe the lie that he will not bother you if you are not bothering him. Do not think that if you kneel before him, he will let you live. Do not think that if you fall, he will show mercy. The enemy does not play by the rules. But do not grow discouraged. Though a righteous man may fall seven times, he will rise again.[13] Therefore, if you fall, choose to get back up. Remember, as a soldier we are to "submit to God. Resist [withstand] the devil, and he will flee."[14] We must continually stand with Christ and against all foes.

## -More than One Enemy-

During wartime, a soldier fights more than one opponent. And in Christ's strength, He empowers us to fight more than one enemy. Think about Theo's adversaries and when the messenger faced off against those two villains who rushed at him. Like the throng of opponents from the story, Paul gives a list of enemies we will encounter: principalities, powers, rulers of the darkness, and spiritual hosts of wickedness. There are many opposing soldiers in this spiritual war, just like in a physical war there are foot soldiers, horsemen, generals, and ruling princes. The same exists in the spirit realm. We are told in Revelation that Satan took a third of the angels with him when he fell and was cast down from heaven.[15] The armies of Satan are indeed real. Scripture also tells us that he makes war against the sons of man, against those who keep the commandments of God and follow Christ.[16] The soldiers of the enemy, those fallen angels, also called demons, torment the inhabitants of the earth. Like the man at the tombs in the gospel of Mark, he was tormented by a legion of demons.[17] A legion is a regiment of over 5,000 men. Along with his legions of demons, we are told Satan roams back and forth across the earth. Like a lion, he seeks those he can devour, and he deceives the whole world.[18] However, we are not doomed to follow in the way of the world, for we know that Christ has overcome the world,[19] and that we, too, can overcome the enemy by the blood of the Lamb and the word of our testimony.[20] Nevertheless, we have to stand firm and endure through the battle against spiritual darkness. David says, "Though an army may encamp against me, my heart shall not fear; though war may rise against me, in [Him] I will be confident."[21] In

Christ we have confidence. Though the whole world turns against us, we can stand in Christ and the power of His word and testimony. Scripture reminds us that "He who is in [us] is greater than he who is in the world."[22] We have been given all the needed strength and armor to withstand the evil one and those who fight with him. Just like the messenger dressed Theo in armor, God dresses us for battle so we can stand and endure enemy attacks. The question is, are we going to succumb to them, or are we going to overcome?

# The Belt of Truth

*"Stand therefore, having girded your waist with truth . . ."*
*- Ephesians 6:14*

In the story, as Theo was dressed for battle, the messenger placed armor on him, beginning with a belt. A soldier is not completely ready for battle until he has been fully armed with all the required equipment. Each piece of armor plays a vital role in our stand against the enemy. Like in the story, each piece serves a purpose. A helmet will protect our head but not our feet; a breastplate covers the chest but not the head; shoes will protect our feet but not our head; and on it goes. The enemy will attack at different levels, and we need to be wearing *all* our armor. Paul did not say pick up only your sword. He said to take up the **whole** armor of God–*all* of it. We are not to pick and choose which we want. We are to put on *all* of it, because we are going to need *all* of it. Once the armor is in place, *then* we are ready to go into the fight, but not before. There are several pieces of armor, but Paul starts with the protection of truth, the belt. He says, "Stand therefore, having girded your waist with truth."[1]

Girded is not a word we often use today, but the word "gird," according to the dictionary, means to bind like with a belt, to encircle, or to surround, and prepare for action. We are to be encircled with Truth. Not relative truths (true for me but not for you), but we are to be encircled with Christ Himself. He is "the way, the *truth*, and the life."[2] He should surround us, and we should cling to Him as if we are bound together. Truth should be so close to us that no one can take it off. Imagine the backbone–strengthening and holding up the rest of the body. If the truth we hold onto is Christ, we will have a strong backbone, but if we take hold of a truth that is twisted, our backbone becomes misshapen. When the backbone is twisted, our body gets out of alignment from its original form, and, eventually, it can no longer hold the body upright.

## -Lies of the Devil-

The enemy does not want strong soldiers for Christ. Therefore, he is going to lie and twist the truth whenever he gets the opportunity. Scripture tells us Satan is the father of lies.[3] He loves to take a piece of truth and twist it to fit his purpose. The devil wants to dislodge and remove our belt and replace it with one of his. If we believe his lies and grasp his partial truths, we are putting on a belt that is warped, frayed, and full of holes. It will fail when the hard times come, and the "truth" you thought you could hold onto is not truth at all. This is how he operates. From the beginning, Satan has been twisting the truth. Look back to Genesis in the Garden of Eden. What did the devil do? He twisted God's words when he asked Eve, "Has God indeed said . . . ?"[4] Twisting and turning like the snake he embodied, Satan played with Eve's mind. His challenge and questioning of God's words incited doubt. He wanted her to doubt the truth she was told by God. Likewise, in Theo's story, the enemy wrote a message hoping to dissuade Theo, causing him to wonder if the King would ever truly come, planting seeds of doubt and despair. And the "truth" of the promises of freedom after surrender was a lie. He would not have let Theo go free, and there would be no peace. The messenger recognized the lies and warned Theo, telling him to hold onto the truth that the King of the Highlands was coming, to stand his ground with his armor on, and keep the truth tightly girded around him. But Theo had to choose whether he would listen and believe the lie or hold fast to truth. In Genesis, Eve chose to listen to Satan's words rather than the truth of God's words. She listened to the wrong voice and trusted the enemy's word instead. She rationalized in her head the lie he fed her. The more she thought about his lie, the more deceived she became. Her focus settled on the temptation. Seeing that the fruit was good and pleasing and desirable for gaining wisdom, she no longer focused on God.[5] She let her belt become lose. Satan had done his work, and she chose to trust the words of a snake instead of her Creator. She let the serpent slither under her armor and separate the truth from its protective hold around her. We cannot let go of truth. But the fight for truth is not just a one-and-done deal. It is an ever-present battle. To fight untruth, we must hold onto *the* Truth.

# -The Enemy in the Garden-

Scripture is full of warnings concerning the attacks of the enemy. The Garden of Eden and the circumstances around the fall of man are excellent examples. To properly fight, it is important to know your enemy. So, what do we know about the serpent? According to scripture, the serpent was "more cunning than any beast of the field."[6] When we look up the definition of cunning, we find the words crafty, sly, and deceit. Such descriptions are like the ones describing the "wiles of the devil" in Ephesians. We also know there is enmity between humanity and the serpent. He will constantly bite our heels causing us to stumble, but we are to crush his head and overcome him.[7] John's book of the Revelation refers to the enemy as the dragon and the "serpent of old, called the Devil," who comes to deceive the whole world.[8] In 2 Corinthians 11:3, Paul fears "as the serpent deceived Eve by his craftiness, so [our] minds may be corrupted." Satan's attack is a ploy against the mind. In Genesis, we note that the serpent is the first one to initiate the conversation. Eve did not seek out the serpent. He waited for an opportune moment to strike. He started the thought process in Eve's mind of desiring something she was not to have. He took her focus off God and placed it on this new desire. Furthermore, he deceptively twisted God's words when he said, "Has God indeed said, 'You shall not eat of every tree in the garden'?"[9] If we look back at chapter two of Genesis, we see what God truly commanded: "And the Lord God commanded the man, saying, 'Of every tree of the garden you may freely eat; but of the tree of the knowledge of good and evil you shall not eat, for in the day that you eat of it you shall surely die."[10] Eve knew the command and clearly told the serpent, "We may eat the fruit of the trees of the garden; but of the fruit of the tree which is in the midst of the garden, God has said, 'You shall not eat, nor shall you touch it, lest you die.'"[11]

Eve knew what was right. However, she did not resist the devil, so he did not flee. Consequently, the longer she listened, the more he lured her away. He discredited God saying, "You will not surely die."[12] The serpent made God sound like a liar and spoke the opposite of what God said, stating, "God knows that in the day you eat of it your eyes will be opened, and you will be like God, knowing good and evil."[13] Along with making God sound like a liar, he appealed to Eve's desire to be like God, to know what was not meant for her to know. He stirred up discontentment, and she just kept listening. He drew her attention away from God and onto herself, saying, "<u>You</u> will be like God." Why would she believe the serpent over God? In retrospect, he had no authority or power over her, and he was in no position to give orders. The enemy did the same thing to Theo. He told Theo the King was not coming, and it would be better for him to surrender. He lied. And as the messenger said, "Do not believe him...the enemy is a liar." He attempted to lead Theo away from the protection of the King. And Satan led Eve down a path of destruction and separation from God. The spiritual connection she had with God broke when she committed the act of disobedience, when she sinned. We must be careful that we do not fall to temptation through listening to the enemy. He may make it sound sweet and pleasing, but when complete, sin bites like a deadly serpent. We must be aware of how the enemy approaches and attacks.

# -The Lure of the World-

The messenger told Theo that the enemy will hold something over you that is desirable, but do not believe the enemy. He is a liar. We must be cautious, for he is very proficient at his deceptions. Satan appealed to Eve's naivete and desire. He tricked her with physical fruit, the promise of mental wisdom, and spiritual authority and power to "be like God." She knew the truth, but she ignored it. She chose what she wanted over what God had said. She was lured in by the lust of the flesh, the lust of the eyes, and the pride of life, as 1 John 2:16 warns. She "saw that the fruit of the tree was good for food" (lust of flesh), "pleasing to the eyes" (lust of the eyes), and "desirable to make [her] wise" (pride of life).[14] John refers to these three areas of attack as the love of the world. We see this same temptation tactic in the New Testament when Satan tempts Christ.[15] Both Christ and Eve were tempted with the same allurements–lust of the flesh, lust of the eyes, and pride of life. Both encountered the enemy and had a choice: fight the enemy or surrender to him. While she started with the truth–"God said..."–Eve did not hold fast to the truth, and she fell captive to the temptations. She kept listening. Christ did not. Christ stood His ground. He responded each time with the Word of God. Sometimes, we are like Eve: we have the right training and start the fight right, but we lose focus and fall at the second or third temptation. Eve did not keep fighting the tempter. She did not flee the temptation. She listened, contemplated them, thought about them, pondered them, wanted them, took them, and then made the thoughts her own and acted–committing the sin. Eve told the serpent the cost and consequence, that disobedience would bring death. Yet, knowing this, she still followed his direction and not that of the Father's. Eve condemned herself. She did not have to listen to or obey the enemy. She had the power and authority to tell him, "No," but instead, she chose to follow and believe the enemy's lie. We do the same thing. We listen to lies and contemplate the twisted truth of it. There is no truth in him. Satan deceives when he speaks his partial truths. He wants to destroy us.

    Just like the stories the messenger told Theo, the enemy wanted to take down the strong man who opposed him, to destroy him and all he loved. Satan wants to separate us from God, from His love, and from His will for our lives. The devil knew the consequences of eating the fruit. Eve told him so. The serpent was trying to get Eve killed and directed her to go after her own destruction, to go to her death. The serpent is still the enemy who wants us to fall. He wants us spiritually dead. The enemy's deceiving enticement may sound good at the time, but it will lead to our downfall. Yet, how can we know? We must test what we hear with truth.

## -Submit to God-

The advice of the enemy is never for our good. If we listen to the enemy, we will fall just as Adam and Eve fell. Their fall led to separation between them and God for all mankind. If we do not humble ourselves, submit to God, ask for forgiveness, turn from evil, resist the devil, and follow God, then, in the end, we will fall from His presence like Adam and Eve did, and it will be an eternal death. Christ states in the book of Matthew concerning those who do not repent but listen to Satan and follow their own way, "Depart from Me, you who practice lawlessness."[16] If we choose to follow the enemy and his direction instead of Christ's direction, we will be cast out like those who are thrown into the furnace where "there will be wailing and gnashing of teeth,"[17] where the fire is never quenched.[18] Nevertheless, if we choose to humble ourselves, submit to God, ask for His forgiveness, turn away from evil, and draw near to God, He is just and faithful to forgive us and welcome us into His presence.[19] We do not have to be deceived and fall like Eve did. We do not have to experience the outcome of the men in the messenger's stories. We are not to be overcome by evil, but we are to overcome evil with good.[20]

# -Girded with Truth-

To fight the lies of the enemy, we need to gird ourselves with the armor of God's truth, be cautious, and hold onto God through it all. When Eve conversed with the enemy, she began with truth, but when the serpent spoke, she did not stop him, and she lost her hold on truth. Christ, on the other hand, was ready for the battle and surrounded Himself with truth. He said again and again, "It is written..."[21] He countered each temptation from Satan with truth. He did not stop to think how good it might feel to eat bread or rule the world–No, He girded Himself with truth and did not give in. He stood His ground. Christ is our example of how to fight the enemy and how to block his attacks. Satan attacked at the most vulnerable time for Christ–when He was hungry and physically weak. Christ was fully human when He faced these attacks. Furthermore, the timing was crucial. Christ was just about to begin His ministry. Up to this point, He had not started healing, teaching, or doing miracles. If Satan could have stopped Christ there, before His ministry began, Satan would have won the fight over humanity permanently. Furthermore, Christ had just spent forty days in the desert with no food. His flesh was hungry. And it was there that Satan made his move. He always attacks the weak points. Yet, his strikes are not immediate death blows. Rather, he manipulatively appeals to the desires of humanity. He does this through the three common areas of attack: lust of the flesh, lust of the eyes, and the pride of life.

# -Lust of the Flesh-

For us to prepare for battle, we must carefully study Jesus, the One who prevailed as Victor over the enemy. Satan's first temptation is an appeal to the flesh through physical hunger. After Christ fasted forty days, scripture says He was hungry.[22] Satan, knowing this, used the hunger as an opportunity to attack, and he laid a trap. However, while Christ fasted, He prayed–which means He was surrounding Himself with the giver of Truth and keeping God as His focus. In a way, He was securing His belt of truth. He was preparing for what was to come. Satan's first attack went straight for the physical desire. Often the weakest part is our physical need and desire for fulfillment. Fulfillment is not a bad desire, but when it consumes us and demands our focus, removing our eyes from the spiritual and placing them on the physical, it can be detrimental for a soldier of Christ. For the longing of fulfillment can distract us from the truth and from the battle. John called this desire lust in 1 John 2:16. Our flesh cries out for fulfillment, and it can be very loud, like the Israelites in the wilderness when they yielded to their craving for meat and complained about the manna, God's bread from heaven.[23] But Christ fought the lust and desire of the flesh and instead looked on the fulfillment of God's will and not His own hunger. Using the natural bodily desire of food, Satan told Christ to turn the stones into bread, an easy thing for Him to do; but the focus of Jesus was not on His hunger, it was on the will of His Father. This is how battles are won! We focus on the Father.

In this attack, Satan fought on two different levels. Level one is aimed at the flesh–a physical attack through hunger. Level two is spiritual; Satan tempted Him, "*If* You are the Son of God. . . ."[24] Satan dares Christ and challenges Christ's power, position, and authority. Looking at the Savior's responses, we can see what the enemy was truly after, his double motive and hidden dagger. Christ responded, "It is written, 'Man shall not live by bread alone, but by every word that proceeds from the mouth of God.'"[25] Christ reiterates what Moses told the Israelite people concerning the manna, that it is God who gives life. God "humbled you, allowed you to hunger, and fed you with manna which you did not know nor did your fathers know, that He might make you know that man shall not live by bread alone; but man lives by every word that proceeds from the mouth of the LORD."[26] It was not just about being physically hungry. It was a power struggle over obedience. It has always been a power struggle. However, Christ used truth to block the attack and did not eat the bread of the enemy but lived by the words of God.

Satan did not suggest Christ turn the stones to bread to satisfy His hunger. Satan suggested it so that Christ would obey and "live" by the words from Satan's mouth and not God's. Satan twisted truth, played mind games, desired Christ's demise, and taunted Him with the phrase, "If You are the Son of God" multiple times. What audacity. He knew who Jesus was, but that did not stop him from trying to gain control over Christ. And knowing we are children of God will not stop him from coming after us. If he went after God in the flesh, you can be sure he will come after us. Satan wanted Christ to fall into the trap of listening to and obeying the enemy. Nevertheless, it did not matter what Satan said, Christ did not yield. Interestingly enough, someone else who wanted Him dead used this same taunt. It was spoken by the scribes and Pharisees at the crucifixion. They called out, "If He is the King" let Him come down.[27] In Luke's account, their chant was, "If He is the Christ."[28] To their taunts, Christ did not yield but kept His eyes on the Father and did the will of the Father. He knew from the beginning of time that He would choose to do the will of the Father. As scripture tells us, "The Lamb [was] slain from the foundation of the world."[29] Jesus knew He would be fighting for His life and ours. Jesus was prepared for battle. He kept His focus where it needed to be. He submitted to God's authority and words of truth, both in the desert fight with Satan and on the cross.

## -Pride of Life-

The second desert attack on Christ was through a twisted version of the truth and an appeal to the pride of life. It was another "if You are" attack. Seeing that Christ fought with scripture, Satan used a different technique. He, too, quoted scripture. Taking Christ up to the pinnacle of the temple,

Satan said to Him, "If You are the Son of God, throw Yourself down. For it is written: 'He shall give His angels charge over You.'"[30] Satan challenges Christ and adds scripture to his taunt, giving a seemingly logical reason to his dare. This maneuver is dangerous to soldiers. And sometimes we fall to this attack. We see the reasoning behind the statement and falter. However, Satan's reasoning is faulty. Like the wicked, deceitful serpent he is, Satan manipulated and twisted God's words from Psalm 91. Satan mocks the scripture and turns it into a dare–tempting Christ to use His power under Satan's command. Looking at Jesus' response, "You shall not tempt the Lord your God," [31] we see Satan's goal was not to see this scripture fulfilled, it was simply to tempt Christ. Satan did not care if Christ hurt His foot, or if the angels would catch Him. Satan just wanted to test God, daring Him to act. You do not do what the enemy says, not when he makes it appear like it's for your own good and certainly not when he dares you. The enemy does not speak the truth. He deceitfully misused scripture in an attempt to destroy Jesus. If we were to keep reading Psalm 91, the chapter that Satan plucked a verse from, we could see that there is a fight, but if God is our refuge, no evil shall befall our souls. The verse following Satan's quote says, "You shall tread upon the lion and the cobra, the young lion and the serpent you shall trample underfoot."[32] Christ's power over Satan is proclaimed in that verse, but when Satan quoted it, he stopped short. He mocked Christ's power and twisted scripture–making it appear as if he had the authority. In reality, Christ has all power and authority.[33] Notice the two creatures Christ treads upon in Psalm 91, the lion and serpent. Satan is described in 1 Peter 5:8 as a lion seeking whom he can devour and in Revelation 20:2 as that ancient serpent of old. Christ's authority from Psalm 91 is over the lion, which is considered the most powerful animal and king of beasts, and the serpent, which is the lowest to the ground yet the most cunning of animals. This described authority from the Psalms portrays Christ's power over all creatures, greatest to smallest, and over all cunning. Yet, to deceive his prey, the enemy leaves off the rest of the scripture and draws attention only to the one part, his partial truth. Satan tempted Christ to listen and obey him, like he did with Adam and Eve. But Christ was prepared for battle. He knew the truth, the word of God. He knew the rest of the scripture. Christ knew what Satan was doing, and He was ready for the attacks. He parried the strike with truth and kept His mind on God.

## -Lust of the Eyes-

As we obey the call to fight, we learn even more by watching Jesus yet again. Satan's third area of attack was appealing to human nature's want for control, power, and riches–a pretentious life (something that pleases man's earthly eyes). The devil offered all the kingdoms of the world. He offered Jesus something physically desirable (not a physical need or an act of daring but something highly appealing to this world). However, Satan was laying a death trap for Christ. He offered a temporary form of power and control, but in reality, he wanted power and control over Christ. Satan offered all the kingdoms of the world to Christ if He would just bow down to him. It was in his authority to offer the kingdoms of the earth;[34] Satan has authority in the world. Yet, when offering a bargain, there are always stipulations with the enemy. He is never offering for anyone's benefit but his own. He wanted control over the Son of God. He wanted worship and power, just like he had before. From the beginning, Satan wanted power and thought himself better than all else. Thus, he was cast down from heaven.[35] He is doing the same thing in Matthew–trying to gain the position that is only God's. He wants God's Son to worship him and change allegiance, obeying his orders and not God's. Hear Christ's response: "Away with you, Satan! For it is written, 'You shall worship the Lord your God, and Him only you shall serve.'"[36]

Jesus knew that Satan offered what was temporary and of this world, not eternal. The enemy offered what seemed the best of what the world had, but Jesus knew it was really a road leading to damnation for the soul. Satan wanted Christ to give up His stance and mission for pleasure and earthly power, to compromise with him. In spiritual warfare, compromising is lethal. Think back to the stories the messenger told. The men all ended up dead or imprisoned with no escape. The enemy does not care for your life. He just wants to take you down, and he will try any means available to him. Satan knew Jesus was the Son of God. He knew that Christ had the power and authority to do what He wanted, but Satan saw in humanity a weakness that we must all choose to overcome, the weakness of the flesh. Satan wanted Christ to compromise and succumb to his rules and authority on earth. But Jesus was prepared to fight. Satan caused humanity to fall once before in Genesis, and he tried to do it again. However, Christ knew the truth, and He held onto it. Even in His humanity, He fought with truth as His guard. He knew that eternity was at stake. This truth helps prepare us for battle as well. Understanding that eternity laid in the balance helped Jesus overcome the temptations and trials of the enemy. This life on earth is not our home but simply a training ground. Our actions and choices on this earth impact where we spend eternity. So, we need to "lay aside every weight, and the sin which so easily ensnares us, and . . . [look] unto Jesus, the author and finisher of our faith;" [37] let us walk in the spirit as Christ did in the desert with eyes focused on the Father. Christ won the fight. Through the temptations, He submitted to God, resisted the devil, and the devil left Him. With Christ living in us, we, too, can do battle and tell the enemy to flee in Jesus' name. If we stand firm in Christ and resist the temptations of the devil, he will flee.[38] Yet, we must be prepared, because it will take perseverance. Satan did not tempt Christ only once; he tried multiple temptations, and after the desert he left for a more opportune time.[39] In Theo's story, the enemy did not stop attacking Theo after the first strike, but continued until one of them overcame. The war we fight is a continual battle, but we are called to fight it. We are to stand firm and resist the enemy, who has no ultimate power. God alone has complete power and authority.

## -Fighting the Flesh-

Satan will portray himself as the one who holds the authority. But know that we overcome by the blood of the Lamb and the word of the testimony. Satan's tactics are not new. He attacks us in the same manner and areas he attacked Christ, which were the same manipulations he used in the garden. The attack through the lust of our flesh, the physical, is one of the easiest ways for the enemy to chip away at our armor and wear us down. The enemy can perceive our needs and desires. He has been observing humanity from the beginning. And as a strategic warrior, he often employs these tactics against us, feeding the desires of our flesh to distract us from the spiritual fight. Scripture tells us that the flesh wars against the spirit, and Satan knows it.[40] Therefore, he feeds the flesh in an attempt to strangle the spirit. The more we dwell on and embrace the passions and longings of the flesh, the more we become like the world and like those of whom Peter speaks as living "for the lusts of men."[41] As Christians, we are to be living for the will of God. If we stand firm, fight against the enemy, and say, "No," if we keep our mind on God and hold His desires above our own, we will be like Christ and able to fight against the devil without failing. This mindset of looking to God is reflected in the Psalms. David, a man of war, wrote on the spiritual war and God's power. He says God "teaches my hands to make war, so that my arms can bend a bow of bronze."[42] He sets my feet upon the rock; "He is my defense; I shall not be moved."[43] These are reflections of the spiritual battle. Only God can enable us to do the impossible, and only God can place us on the Spiritual Rock, Christ.

Isaiah the prophet also speaks of this spiritual battle and the spiritual renewing that only God can give. He lifts us up on wings like eagles and renews our strength.[44] It is through Christ and the power of God that we can stand and fight the enemy, but we must choose to focus on the spiritual battle and not be caught in the desires of the physical. Paul says those that are Christ's have "crucified the flesh" and are to live and "walk in the spirit."[45] Having crucified the flesh is not something done *to* them, or *for* them but *by* them. This is not physical but spiritual. It is a choice. We must choose to put to death our fleshly desires.

And what if, God forbid, I lose my focus and fall? Am I forever lost? The book of Proverbs says though the righteous fall seven times, they get back up.[46] When we fall, we must repent and get back on our feet. Reset your focus on the battle and the One who is within you. And do not, as Paul says, grow weary of doing good.[47] We cannot stop fighting the enemy; if we do, he wins. It is as the messenger told Theo: the war does not stop. We fight for as long as we are able, for as long as we have strength, for as long as we have breath. So, do not lie fallen in filth and sin. Get up and fight victoriously.

## -Conquering Pride-

Satan attacks through the pride of life, a selfish pride where you glory in yourself and what you have done or how great you are. This pride is what Paul warns against in 1 Timothy 3:6 "lest being puffed up with pride he [man] fall into the same condemnation as the devil." Paul knew there would be the temptation of pride. As there was in the beginning, and again with Christ, Satan draws the church away in the same manner. Pride is a very dangerous characteristic and one that is not beneficial for us. Not only does scripture tell us that pride was Satan's downfall,[48] but that "everyone proud in heart is an abomination to the Lord."[49] Pride was the downfall of Herod in Acts 12:21-23. When people flattered Herod, saying he was a god, he did not humble himself and turn the praise to the only true God. Instead, he gloried in it. Therefore, God sent an angel to strike him down.

He died from the inside out, the way pride is born, which is also the way of sin. It begins on the inside.

To conquer pride, we must remain humble. James says the Lord resists the proud but gives grace to the humble.[50] And this verse is followed by submitting to God and resisting the devil. It is all about the spiritual battle and how we are to fight it. Humility is the spiritual block to the attack of pride. But it must be exercised and put into practice. However, we must not become proud of our humility. We must be careful not to get caught in the trap of thinking we know more or better than God or that we can conquer the enemy in our own power and ability. The messenger told Theo his focus was in the wrong place when they talked after he was wounded. He was focusing on his own power, and if he leaned on this own strength, or even that of others, it would not be strong enough, and he would fail. Our focus must be on God. Our humility before His authority is vital.

# -Keeping Eyes Focused-

Along with pride, there is the attack through the lust of the eyes. The lust of the eyes could be desire for wealth, people, visual stimulation, allurements, and things that entice us. It is a visual desire. Satan wants to distract our eyes, for the eyes are like a window to the soul. If he can catch our eyes and focus them on lusts and desires, then he distracts our souls from focusing on God. Christ describes it as the eyes being a lamp to the body. Through them we bring either light or darkness to our souls.[51] Whatever we focus on is what we fight for. It is a dangerous battle we are fighting. The messenger told Theo, "The enemy holds ransom something we want . . . but no matter the situation, we cannot compromise. Compromising is lethal." The enemy wants us to desire luxury, to compromise our morality, to look to the things of the world and bend to his limited will, not the Lord's eternal will. This may seem pleasurable in the moment, but the end cost is detrimental, like the man who was locked in the room with the gold. Satan offers us something we can see, but we often fail to see the costs, consequences, and agony it causes our spirit both now and in the future. When we lose focus of Christ, of the Truth, we get consumed in the natural desires of the flesh. Satan knows in the end that if we stay holding on to the truth of Christ, we will reign *with* Christ, but he also knows that the lust of the eyes and desires of the flesh are very powerful and tempting. Wanting to deter us from heaven, the devil offers visual pleasures and momentary stimulation in exchange for our souls. We must choose, as Theo did with the note, to crumble the threat of the enemy and stand and fight.

## -Follow Christ's Example-

The messenger asked Theo, "What will you choose?" We all have choices to make. No one is perfect, but we, as Christians, are called to follow in the footsteps of Christ. He was, and He remains, sinless. This does not mean we will not make mistakes. It means we are to try our utmost to walk worthy of the calling of Christ. However, when we fall, society tends to say, "We are all human, and we all make mistakes." While that is true, it is not to be used as an excuse. Christ was human and had the same inner struggles we have.[52] Yet, through the temptations, trials, and attacks, He did not fall. He is our example to follow. He is the One we are to imitate. Peter writes that Christ left us "an example, that [we] should follow His steps."[53] Paul tells the church in Corinth, "Imitate me, just as I also imitate Christ."[54] Jesus said, "If anyone desires to come after Me, let him deny himself, and take up his cross, and follow Me."[55] We are to follow after Him in every way, especially in the way He battled the enemy. Jesus used truth to block all Satan's attacks. He stood strong in God and did what was right. He did not walk in the path of the Deceiver. He did not play mind games or rationalize the lies of the enemy. He held on to truth, knowing and trusting

God's words over all others. He did not allow his mind to dwell on the enemy's allurements or temptations. He did not let His guard down. He did not grow angry and forfeit His peace. He trusted God's promises and commands. He spoke truth. He kept His mind focused. He did not fall. He held on to God. With Christ as our example, we, too, are to stand with truth cinched securely around us.

## -Get Up and Learn-

However, if we do fall, for there are times we do, we cannot undo or go back, but we can choose to get up and set our mind for what to do in the future. Like the messenger told Theo, "Let us learn from our mistakes" and gain strength. If we fall, we must get back up and fight again. The book of Proverbs informs us that although the righteous fall seven times, he will get back up.[56] However, life will not be the same. There are consequences for our actions. For Adam and Eve, Adam had to till the ground, Eve would have pain in childbirth, and they had to leave the garden. Nevertheless, while the consequences remained, when they repented, God had mercy on them. And God in His mercy and grace is willing to forgive us if we repent, turn to Him, and no longer walk in sin.[57] But repentance is a choice, and fighting the enemy is a choice. We must fight our desires, fight against the temptations of the enemy, and hold tightly to the truth of Christ. We must wrap that spiritual belt around us. Not just for today, not just for tomorrow, but for all our lives. We are to learn from the Truth, the examples of scripture, and realize it is not just the beginning of the fight that matters. We must stand strong through it all. We are to endure to the end.[58] Are you willing to hold on to God's truth and continue the fight?

# The Breastplate of Righteousness

*". . . Having put on the breastplate of righteousness. . ." - Ephesians 6:14*

In the story, the messenger instructs Theo to put on a breastplate. Paul instructs the soldiers of Christ to "put on the breastplate of righteousness." Historically, breastplates were sections of metal plates formed to protect the upper body, covering the torso, which contained the vital organs, especially the heart. The heart is an essential organ. It is what keeps us alive. The heart pumps blood throughout the entire body. Therefore, Paul's directions must be heeded. For if the enemy can take the heart, he has won the battle. If the enemy can strike the heart, he can destroy the rest of the body. If he can pierce the heart with a poison arrow by filling it with lies, the rest of us will become poisoned. If he cannot strike the heart, he will aim for other essential areas. A wounded lung or a pierced gut is very painful and can be detrimental. However, his first attack will be at the heart. The heart or soul, spiritually speaking, is a facilitator directing the rest of the body. When the heart is full of joy, it brings strength to the body. However, if our heart is full of depression or worry, it will fill the body and cause decay in our lives. The book of Proverbs tells us that a broken spirit dries up the bones.[1] The enemy wants to dry up our bones and destroy our lives, but we must fight him. We must guard our hearts from the attacks of the enemy. Like the messenger told Theo, killing you is his goal, but wounding you is to his advantage. Therefore, we must take up arms and guard ourselves with the breastplate of righteousness.

# -Prepare-

To rightfully prepare, we are to fill our hearts and souls with what is right–to align ourselves with God and His word. Philippians gives a list of attributes on which to focus and set our minds. We are to think on things that are pure, noble, lovely, of good report, true, and right.[2] These traits help us care for our heart, protecting it and strengthening it. Regarding a battle, our minds must be set on doing what is right. We must choose what stance we are going to take and if we are going to remain dedicated to finishing the fight. If our souls are not dedicated to the fight, we will lose the ability to continue, and we will not win. The man who surrendered to the enemy was not dedicated to the fight. In fact, he was trying to avoid the fight and pain that would come. However, the fight is not something we can avoid. We can close our eyes to it and suffer, or we can stand and fight. It is ever present and ever waging. We are given the armor with which to protect ourselves, and the breastplate of righteousness is an essential piece.

In our world, the enemy has slipped a dagger under the breastplate of humanity. He has deceived people into choosing evil and turning away from righteousness. He has deceived the world by corrupting their morals–turning what is right into things deemed to be wrong, and he has turned what is wrong into what is deemed acceptable and good. Do not be deceived. Satan roams about seeking those he can devour, searching for hearts he can destroy. The corruption of society is not an accident–it is a war tactic, and we must not fall victim to the world's twisted logic and lies. Paul tells Timothy that evil will always be present and will grow worse, but we are to hold tightly to what the scriptures have taught us,[3] that "all who desire to live godly [righteously] in Christ Jesus will suffer persecution."[4] There will be war. We are not to quit the battle, and we are not to give in to the pressures of the world. As the messenger warned Theo of the ploys of the enemy, Paul warns us and cautions us to be aware and on guard. The world will make it look appealing and everyone else might be doing it, but we are called to a higher standard. Jesus tells us, "To whom much is given, from him much will be required." [5]We are called to give up the things of this world and follow Christ.

## -Walk Righteously-

We are not put here on earth to walk in the ways of the flesh, to follow the world and worldly desires. We are to be filled with the Holy Spirit and walk in righteousness according to the Spirit. This life is our training ground, just like Theo had to train before the victory came. As soldiers of Christ, part of our training is to "do all things without complaining and disputing, that [we] may become blameless and [pure], children of God without fault in the midst of a crooked and perverse generation, among whom [we] shine as lights in the world, holding fast the word of life."[6] If we hold fast to Christ and follow His example in obedience, our good works will shine like lights in the world. People will see and watch. Will the light fade and be overtaken by the dark, or will it remain a steadfast beacon for others to see? Our works of righteousness, our lives, are seen by others. Psalm 37:6 says, God "shall bring forth your righteousness as the light, and your justice as the noonday." He is there fighting with you, strengthening you. He is bringing righteousness to the light and letting justice shine. He fights for you. And when we walk in the righteousness of God, we will shine like a light. It may not be visible in the physical world, but in the spiritual world righteousness is evident, just like light is evident in the darkness.

## -Hold Fast-

However, when we put on the breastplate of righteousness, we must be ready. Never forget that the darkness hates the light. Therefore, the enemy will do whatever he can to destroy the light. He will attack us, poison us, deceive us, and try to destroy the light within us. If the enemy can poison the heart and mind, the rest of the body will follow, ending in a painful, eternal death. But we must stand strong and hold fast to Christ. We must fight evil with God's righteousness. His righteousness must surround our hearts so we can withstand the enemy's attacks. And what if the enemy strikes us elsewhere, on the side or in the gut? We continue to fight. It is true he wants to kill the heart, but if he cannot, he will attempt to wound us elsewhere, anywhere he can pierce us. If the enemy cannot take the castle by the first maneuver, then he will try another approach. The enemy first sent a spy dressed as a beggar, hoping to gain entrance. When that tactic failed, he tried another. If he cannot pierce the heart, the enemy will strike other vital organs. Similarly, in our lives, if the enemy cannot destroy us because we are standing firm, he will attack those around us, those we love and care for, and fellow soldiers. Remember the man with the family. The enemy used those he loved to gain control. He will attack the home and the workplace. He knows where to attack. He knows wounds will make us weak and exhausted. And if we do not continue to stand against him, the enemy will overcome. But scripture tells us, "Do not be overcome by evil, but overcome evil with good," that is, with righteousness.[7] When we act righteously, we stand guard against the attacks of the enemy. This does not mean we are invincible or that we will never be struck, but it means we are able to stand against the attacks and live. We fight the wiles of the enemy and stand our guard against his schemes and poison.

## -Be Diligent-

In the book of Proverbs, we learn that we are to guard our hearts with all diligence.[8] A soldier must be diligent to put on his armor and breastplate every day. To guard our hearts and walk in His righteousness, we have to put aside anything that might hinder or weigh us down. We must act as the writer of Hebrews tells us and "lay aside every weight . . . which so easily ensnares us."[9] We must give over our worries, fears, and desires to God. A soldier cannot fight properly when he is weighed down by burdens. They will hinder his movements, deplete his strength, and cause his mind to be occupied with the weight and not with the fight. We must give God everything–the good and the bad, fears and dreams, horrors and hopes, independence and families, freedom and control, plans and lives. If we hold anything back, we are not letting God have complete control. If we try to lean on our own understanding and do not relinquish control to God, we will fall as Theo did in the battle when he trusted in his own ability and strength. In the book of Proverbs, we read: "Trust in the Lord with all your heart, and lean not on your own understanding."[10] God gives us what we need for each battle, and He expects us to use the armor He has provided. We are to trust His judgment and commands. He knows the plans He has for us. They are plans for our good, plans for a hope and a future.[11] But before we can reach that heavenly hope and future, we must prevail in the fights against sin and the enemy. To do that, we must use our armor correctly, we cannot have anything else hindering us from the fight. We must lay aside the weights of this world and press on towards the goal, to finish by fighting the good fight.

Paul tells Timothy, "No one engaged in warfare entangles himself with the affairs of this life, that he may please him who enlisted him as a soldier."[12] A soldier is focused. His walk is that of discipline and determination. His mind is on what lies ahead, and his goal is to please the one who enlisted him for service. As Christian soldiers, our walk is to resemble that of Christ. We are to walk in love, which will result in walking righteously. To the observer, our walk, our lifestyle, and choices are like banners before an army. We proclaim our colors and the One we serve. Our lives are to proclaim the praises of Christ and the Father. But scripture warns us that those who do not walk righteously, those who love the world, are not of the Father.[13] Therefore, if we are to be like the Father and like Christ, we must resist rather than imitate the rest of the world. It is hard, but it is true. Theo had the choice. He could give into the enemy's demands, or he could stand and fight against him. It would be hard, but it would be worth it. Remember what the messenger said: "In many battles, the enemy holds ransom something we want." We must resist the urge to compromise and stay focused on the battle. For our enlistment is not for ourselves but for God and His service. We must be on guard. Today, we can easily become distracted by things that we want, things the world has to offer. But the world is not our friend. This is a ploy of the enemy. It may not be a frontal attack, but it may be a spy at the door, or a knife to the side. The desires of the world are an ally of the devil. He will use them to distract us from the fight and away from righteousness. James warns us how even friendship with the world is enmity with God. Enmity is defined as a condition of hostility, hatred, ill will, antagonism, and an opposing force. According to James, those who want to make themselves a friend of the world make themselves an enemy of God.[14] John says, "Do not love the world or the things in the world. If anyone loves the world, the love of the Father is not in him."[15] The world holds no righteousness. The world does not accept Christ. The world hates and is at war with Christ, and it wars with those who follow Him.[16] We are to train as soldiers and fight, not succumb to and be like the world but to be set apart from it and stand against its wiles. We are called to be one with the Father,[17] and the things of the world are not of the Father.[18] We know He is righteous, and those who practice righteousness are born of Him, and those who do righteousness are righteous, just as He is righteous.[19] But those who practice lawlessness will be told to depart from Him. Christ will tell them, "I never knew you."[20] Our orders are to follow Christ, to stand with Him and against those who oppose Him. And when the world opposes Him, we are to stand and fight. Therefore, to avoid being swayed and caught in the temptations of the world, we must immerse ourselves in the things of Christ. So, when others look at us, they see the light of Christ. They see Him in our words, actions, and examples. Jesus said in Matthew's Gospel to let your light shine so that others would see and glorify our Father in heaven.[21] The righteousness of God is to shine through us. If others do not see Christ, if we do not see Christ within, we need to reexamine ourselves. Ask yourself, "Am I putting Christ first in everything? Does my light shine so that God is seen and glorified? Is God's righteousness evident in my life?"

# -Evidence of Christ-

When Theo first meets the messenger, it is apparent that he is from the King. He wore the King's colors and spoke the words of the King. As Christians, there is to be evidence in our lives that we belong to the King of heaven, the King above all kings. There are certain character qualities we should display and certain standards we are called to uphold. Scripture is filled with examples of virtues and characteristics we are to exhibit along with guidance of what to avoid and what to pursue. We are to walk in humility,[22] love,[23] and obedience.[24] We are to "abhor what is evil. Cling to what is good."[25] We are to "flee youthful lusts" and "pursue righteousness, faith, love, peace with those who call on the Lord out of a pure heart."[26] We are to purify ourselves as Christ is pure.[27] We are to have a servant's heart as Christ did.[28] The righteousness of God within us is evident by the fruit of the Spirit in our lives: love, joy, peace, patience, kindness, goodness, gentleness, faithfulness, and self-control.[29] We are to walk in the Spirit and "not fulfill the lust of the flesh."[30] In fact, the epistle to the Galatians informs us that if we are Christ's, we are to crucify "the flesh with its passions and desires."[31] This is a daily decision to walk righteously, and each soldier must make his or her own decision. Theo had to decide if he was going to stand against evil or give up the fight. He had many opportunities to decide, and with each moment of our lives, we get to make the same decision.

# -Transformed Minds-

To walk righteously, we need to walk in the Spirit. Paul says we are to be transformed by the renewing of our minds.[32] Our minds are to be transformed. No longer are we to desire the things of this world, but we are to desire Christ. We are not to focus on the temporary but rather on the eternal. Theo and the men in the stories were focused on the moment, on the physical, what was right before them. The two men did not consider the lasting impact of their decisions. Theo, too, stood face-to-face with the moment, but the messenger helped him to see beyond the here and now and to trust the King, even when he could not see the outcome. Christ asks the same of us. Do not be transfixed on the physical here and now but look toward the goal. Even when we cannot see what lies ahead, we can place it in the hands of Jesus and walk in obedience as a good soldier of Christ. We can keep our minds ready for battle and not become distracted by the things of this world. Remember what Christ said in Matthew's Gospel, chapter six: He cares for us like the lilies of the field and the birds of the air. He provides for all our needs.[33] So, while living in the Spirit, trust God with the physical and do not be consumed by the cares of the world. We are to be focused on the things of God, the things of the Spirit. Paul says, "the kingdom of God is not eating and drinking, but righteousness and peace and joy in the Holy Spirit."[34] The physical and its pleasures will not endure. They are here one day and gone the next, but righteousness, peace, and joy are everlasting. Christ gives us His peace,[35] and the Holy Spirit gives us help and guides us in righteousness. If we follow and obey, it will be evident in our lives and last through eternity. When we walk in the Holy Spirit, He will point us to Christ, reminding us of Him and His words.[36] The Holy Spirit constantly guides, convicts, and directs us to Christ, and Christ directs us to the Father. Our minds are to focus on Him. Psalm 89:14 states, "Righteousness and justice are the foundation of [His] throne; mercy and truth go before [His] face." If the foundation of God's throne is righteousness, then that should be the foundation of our lives, and if mercy and truth are ever before His face, then that is what we should keep before our face and in our minds. We are to focus on God, to look for His mercy and truth, and to walk in His righteousness. Scripture teaches us to "do justly, to love mercy, and to walk humbly with [our] God."[37] We set our minds on things above, not on the things of this world.[38] Paul said that we, too, were once of the worldly mindset–but no longer.[39] We must spiritually put to death our old man and live as a new man, made alive in Christ for the glory of the Father. It is time to let His righteousness shine through us and guard our hearts.

## -The Heart Matters-

Scripture says the Lord tests the hearts of men.[40] He is searching for those who are faithful, those who, like David, have a heart after His own.[41] When Samuel looked at the sons of Jesse, seeking God's choice to anoint as king, God informed Samuel that while "man looks at the outward appearance... the Lord looks at the heart."[42] The appearance of man is not what matters, but what is in the heart is what matters. As Christ told the Pharisees, it is not what goes into a man that defiles him, but what comes out of him, out of his heart.[43] As good soldiers, we are to check our own hearts and see if we line up with Christ. We are to be like David when he says, "create in me a clean heart, O God, and renew a [right] spirit within me."[44] We want our hearts to be clean, pure, and righteousness before God. David says in Psalm 139, "Search me, O God, and know my heart; try me, and know my [thoughts]; and see if there is any wicked way in me, and lead me in the way of everlasting."[45] David is asking God to test him, to search his heart, to point out any wrongs inside of him. He is humbly submitting himself to the corrections of God as a good soldier. Let us also seek God in such a way. Ask Him to show us our faults and wickedness that we may be washed anew and be righteous before Him. Once the heart is clean, the body becomes clean, and it can be strengthened in righteousness, and as the heart strengthens, so does the rest of the body.

## -Evidence in Fruit-

We must fill ourselves with Christ. We must draw near to God and spend time with Him and in His Word. The evidence is in the Spirit working in us which is seen by the fruit of the Spirit in our lives–love, joy, peace, patience, kindness, goodness, gentleness, faithfulness, and self-control. Jesus said, "a tree is known by its fruit,"[46] and "every good tree bears good fruit."[47] However, if the evidence in my life does not portray those characteristics, then am I truly drawing near to God, or am I drawing near to the world? Are my actions righteous? John said those who practice righteousness are of the Father, those who do not are not of the Father.[48] They are consumed with the world.

The world is full of hatred, abuse, lies, destruction, and wars. It is not something we want to be part of. Yet, if we allow ourselves to be drawn near to the world, we let darkness drown out our light, and as darkness fills us, righteousness leaves us. We cannot be one with the world and one with God. A soldier cannot fight for and against his King. We must choose where to stand and what to fight against. We must put on the breastplate of righteousness and protect our heart, our selves, from the evil one. Whatever we focus on and draw near to is what we will become like. If we draw near to the world, we fill ourselves with things of the world, with malice, hatred, dissensions, envy, anger, strife, and impurity.[49] It will become evident. For example, when the Pharisees said they were sons of Abraham, Jesus said Abraham looked forward to seeing Him, but they were children of the devil.[50] They did not know Christ, nor did they know the Father. They did not draw near to God like Abraham did. Their fruit was evil, and they pulled away from God and drew near to themselves, like Satan did. Outwardly, they appeared "righteous to men, but inside [they were] full of hypocrisy and lawlessness."[51] We do not want to follow the example of the Pharisees walking in the way of the world, letting darkness creep in and cover us. We want to follow the examples of those who were righteous. The righteous ones of the past like Abel,[52] Noah,[53] and Abraham,[54] and those who followed Christ as the apostles did, listening to and dwelling on His teachings, drawing near to Him. Scripture says when others heard the disciples, they knew "they had been with Jesus."[55] It was evident in their lives. Is it evident in our lives? We want others to know that we have been with Jesus. Let our lives shine as lights and evidence of His righteousness.

## -Right Standing-

Righteousness is right standing, doing what is right. When we do what is right, we secure the breastplate. The stronger the breastplate, the harder it will be for the enemy to penetrate and poison the heart. But be warned; as God strengthens you, the enemy will try to invade and break through your breastplate. If he cannot reach the heart, he will aim for other organs. Though the heart is the goal, the poisoning of other organs is very painful and serves his purpose of attack, weakening you, disarming you, and distracting you. If he can get us to focus on the pain and forget about the battle, he has gained a victory. When Theo was struck by the enemy, the pain nearly cost him the fight, not to mention his life. His focus was on the hurt and agony. The enemy had not killed him yet. He had only wounded him. However, Theo had to remain standing to win the battle. He had to do what was right as a soldier in the King's army. As soldiers in God's army, we, too, must choose to stand and fight, to do what is right, even when we are in great pain. The fight does not stop when we are wounded. It will continue. Paul said that though he was struck down, he was not destroyed.[56] The enemy may strike us, but he will not destroy us if we remain in right standing before God and keep our breastplate of righteousness and armor secure. Scripture says, "Be watchful, and strengthen the things which remain."[57] When wounded in battle, it is important that we strengthen that which remains; focus our minds on God and our energy on the fight. No matter what the enemy does, we must purpose in our hearts and minds to stand with the breastplate of righteousness securely in its place. We are His soldiers, called by Him to fight the darkness. As soldiers in His army, we put on righteousness as a breastplate so that when the enemy attacks and tries to poison us, we stand pure and upright before the Lord and fight this enemy of our soul.

# The Shoes of Preparation and Peace

*"And having shod your feet with the preparation of the gospel of peace."*
*- Ephesians 6:15*

In the story, the messenger instructs Theo to put on battle shoes. Paul tells us our feet must be shod with "the preparation of the gospel of peace." Shod, simply put, means to put on shoes. In Roman times, the soldiers' shoes consisted of sandals with leather straps that tied around their feet and ankles. On the bottom of the shoes were small spikes that pressed into the ground. This enabled a soldier to stand firm. He would not slip in the rain or mud. He was prepared to hold his position or to advance without fear.

As we walk through life, we will encounter spiritual mudslides, hardships, trials, and persecution from the enemy. Knowing these obstacles are ahead can be terrifying, but it also helps us prepare. The fear of hardship or battle must not stop us from the fight. When we strap on the shoes of peace, we surrender our fears to God. We unburden ourselves to the Lord, release, let go of our concerns, and trust in Him. As good soldiers, we are to seek first the Kingdom of God. If our feet are firmly placed in God, we can encounter whatever comes against us. Theo saw the enemy camped outside and knew they would attack, but the messenger told him also used in place of the word preparation. To prepare is to make ready. To have zeal is to be enthusiastically dedicated to a cause, to have dedication with a fierce determination, that no matter what, we will persevere. We must be dedicated to finish the fight, and we must ready ourselves for the battles ahead. Do not be deceived. The shoes of the preparation of the gospel of peace enable us to stand and endure through the battles. Paul's dedication and determination to stand as a soldier of God led him through many battles after his conversion to Christ Jesus. He was imprisoned in Jerusalem, put under house arrest in Rome, and placed in a Roman prison before being taken before Caesar for prosecution. Through all these trials and spiritual battles, Paul stood his ground. He was prepared for the work ahead of him like a good soldier, knowing that it was God who made the way, and in Him was true victory. In the book of John, Jesus is described as having a zeal for the house of the Lord that is consuming.[5] It is demanding and calling His soldiers to action. We are to have desire and determination to do right and fight for God. No matter what comes our way, we can be like the messenger and Theo and stand against the armies of the enemy.

We must prepare our minds and not let ourselves be deceived or caught off guard by the enemy's imitation of peace, but we must fight against his schemes. The illusion of the enemy will not sustain you in battle nor will it strengthen you to endure what lies ahead. Beware, when we are exhausted, the devil can easily step in and offer us a mirage of peace. Fighting a battle wears a soldier down, and during war, soldiers long for peace. We tire of the struggle and desire to escape it, so we often settle for a temporary peace, something that deters or distracts our minds and brings us pleasure. But when we return to the battlefield, we are not rested. We are more worn down than before, and all we want to do is escape again. This is what the enemy wants. He is quick to offer a diversion from the fight. He constantly tries to remove us from the battle. He wants our minds off the truth and on other things so we will lay down our armor. The enemy's offer of peace and escape is not enduring. It is a distraction from the truth, and the peace or pleasure it may bring is fleeting. True peace only comes from God, and He gives it to us when we determine within ourselves to fight for Him. He does not take us out of the battle. He strengthens us through the fight. His peace does not drain us but enables us to continue.

People crave peace and are constantly trying to gain peace, but too often they search for peace in the wrong places. The man whose family was imprisoned by the enemy thought he could gain peace for his loved ones, but he trusted in the wrong place. He surrendered to the duplicity of the enemy and found the opposite of peace. Peace does not come from the enemy, or from outside sources. Peace comes from God. Christ said, "My peace I give to you; not as the world gives do I give to you."[6] The world gives a pretense of peace but only at the cost of something too great–our enlistment as God's soldiers. If we are not careful, we will fall into the trap of the enemy and his proposed peace. If we surrender to the wrong side, we will be like the man who lost everything and gained nothing.

## -The World's Peace-

To gain the world's temporary peace, it requires us to give up our standards as a soldier of Christ, to lay down our armor and surrender. But to surrender to the world is to give up our armor and source of defense. Remember the army that surrendered. They gave up their weapons and were slaughtered by the enemy. For soldiers, to surrender in a spiritual war is to sign their own execution orders. Yet, so often in our pursuit of peace, we negotiate with the world, surrender, and agree to its demands. Bending a knee to its will, we hope for peace, not knowing that the peace we are searching for does not exist in the world. The men from the examples that the messenger gave did not know that what the enemy offered would bring death. They thought it was a way out. As the messenger said to Theo, the enemy "might make it sound appealing, but do not believe him. There is no peace where he is concerned." But often, we become deceived and lay down our armor. We surrender to the pressures of the world in hopes of attaining peace. Pilate is an example of a soldier who surrendered to the wrong side. The Pharisees, when shouting for the crucifixion of Christ, told Pilate he was not a friend of Caesar if he let Jesus live.[7] Pilate did not want to crucify Him, knowing that He had done nothing deserving of death.[8] Yet, Pilate succumbed to the pressures of the world. In hopes of peace, and not wanting the rioting to reach Caesar, Pilate surrendered his stand and laid down his armor to calm the masses. He ordered and exchanged the crucifixion of Christ for temporary peace that did not last. Like the enemy's letter to Theo, Pilate was offered peace if he would surrender and give up the fight. But there is no peace where the world is involved. It is vital that as soldiers of Christ we do not compromise on truth to gain temporary peace with the world. We must prepare and keep our minds focused on the fight. We must plant our feet and stand firm. With those spikes on our shoes, we dig into the ground, hold onto our foundation, and fight. We must resist the enemy. Often, we focus on having a good time and ignore the fight. We hide from confrontation and seek to please. But if we focus on the cares of the world, we will surrender to the enemy. We want peace, which is good and desirable, but the truth is that in the middle of a perverse, twisted, and godless generation, there is no peace. The world does not accept Christ, and it will not do the will of the Father. Metaphorically and spiritually speaking, the world wants those who follow Christ to surrender, to give up God's peace, and to become like them. But if a soldier lays down his armor during a battle and surrenders to the will and pressures of the enemy, it is spiritual death.

The enemy will tell you to align yourself with him to gain peace. He will say as he did to Theo, "This fight is strenuous . . . let us stop this unnecessary pain." But as the messenger said, the enemy "offers an illusion of true peace, but it will never be." The apostles were given an ultimatum–preach Christ and be imprisoned and beaten, or refrain and the Pharisees would leave them alone.[9] The Pharisees offered a treaty, but their peace was based on fear and control. The world claims peace when underneath it is unstable fear. And if fear is not working, the enemy reverts to simple illusions and distractions of peace. Society creates a rush and a 'make the most environment,' promoting peace or satisfaction. But the so-called peace of reaching such goals is fleeting or nonexistent. It does not strengthen us or last, and we find ourselves discontent. Everyone must get the newest technology, car, or fashion. People market articles of this world with the pretense of fulfillment and happiness. Yet, once it is in our grasp, all we want is more. The world's peace and satisfaction do not exist, for in true peace there is contentment. The enemy has caused humanity to chase fantasies instead of truth.[10] Ezekiel warns of those who double-cross others, how they proclaim, "'Peace!' when there is no peace."[11] Isaiah says, "The way of peace they have not known, and there is no justice in their ways. They have made themselves crooked paths; [and] whoever takes that way shall not know peace."[12] The world does not know peace, and those who follow the world lose peace. They become more anxious, greedier, and more deceived. We should not be surprised at this tactic of the enemy. Like Theo, when the enemy offers a truce, it sounds alluring, but his intent is against you, trying to deceive you to give up the fight and eternal victory. He will never cease pursuing the children of God. As the messenger said, the enemy will not stop deceiving and attacking "until they are completely destroyed." Our battle will not end until Jesus returns and destroys the darkness.

## -Peace in Persecution-

The war here is ever raging. Scripture forewarns us that the world will hate us if we follow Jesus, and that we will suffer persecution.[13] Christ said, if they persecuted Me, they will persecute you.[14] In the sermon on the mount, He spoke blessings for those who would be persecuted for righteousness' sake and those who would be persecuted for His name's sake.[15] To Timothy, Paul writes, "all who desire to live godly in Christ Jesus will suffer persecution."[16] Persecution does not mean a lack of peace. It means personal attacks. There will be hardships. But amid persecution lies a miracle of peace–if our eyes remain focused on Christ. Persecution is nothing new. According to history, when the apostle Andrew was on trial for his life, he was told to stop preaching Christ or be crucified. Andrew responded, "I would not have preached the honor and glory of the cross if I feared the death of the cross."[17] He was killed for his stand, yet he was prepared to fight and die for Christ. His feet were firmly planted in the peace of God. Paul says to live is Christ, and to die is gain.[18] He means we are to live for Christ as His soldiers, and if we die as His soldiers, then it is gain, for we go to be with Christ in heaven. Paul's words are an example of the peace that soldiers of God can have. Live or die; it does not matter. Our peace is not from this world but from Christ. Paul, in the book of Acts, encourages the believers that we must go through suffering and tribulation to enter the kingdom.[19] This is not to discourage them but to prepare and encourage them. Paul knew about persecution. He endured a stoning that was meant to kill him. Yet, he got back up, and he did not fear. As a good soldier, he continued to fight until he was beheaded for following Christ. When we are persecuted for following Him, like Andrew and Paul, we choose to lay aside our own lives. Jesus said, "he who does not take his cross and follow after Me is not worthy of Me."[20] We must prepare our hearts and minds for persecution and be zealous and dedicated to Christ. Fight against the enemy and live in a manner worthy of Christ. Fight as soldiers of God.

## -Do Not Fear-

We must not fear. We must not fear men, nor should we fear death. Jesus told His disciples not to fear the man who can kill the body, but the Lord who judges the soul and has power over hell.[21] In the story, the messenger did not fear the enemy or his threats. He was ready to face whatever lay before him. He told Theo that he must choose, but as for himself, the messenger said, "I choose to stand and follow my King." For those in the story, the war started when the enemy turned against the King. He was cast out of the kingdom, yet he continued to frighten, attack, and torment the King's subjects. The spiritual war we are in has been going on since before the creation of the world. Adam and Eve were the first soldiers to guard a castle. And it is our turn to continue the fight. Do not fear. Only one side comes out victorious, and that is God's side. 2 Corinthians 2:14 says, "Now thanks be to God who always leads us in triumph in Christ, and through us diffuses the fragrance of His knowledge in every place." In the battle, Christ leads us in triumph against the schemes of Satan, but victory is not something that just happens. It must be fought for. Triumph only comes after a trial. Therefore, do not fear temporary persecution, because in the end we stand with our King in eternal victory and peace.

## -The Peace of Christ-

Christ's peace is not like the world's. His peace is what the psalmist describes in Psalm twenty-three, "He leads me beside still waters. He restores my soul; He leads me in the paths of righteousness for His name's sake. Yea, though I walk through the valley of the shadow of death, I will fear no evil; for You are with me; Your rod and Your staff, they comfort me. You prepare a table before me in the presence of my enemies."[22] God's peace enables us to walk through the shadow of death, to sit down and eat in the presence of the enemy, and not be afraid. It is a peace that enables us to walk through the trials and hardships of battle, a peace that gives us the strength to endure. His peace surpasses all understanding.[23] There are firsthand accounts of persecuted Christians in our lifetime who were filled with joy and peace while held in a prison cell. It made no sense to those watching. But God is not limited to the world's understanding. The messenger told Theo, "Do not be afraid... You have been given a strength that none can truly comprehend." This unseen strength and peace will come to light when the battles grow stronger. That is when the enemy and those around you see your strength. In the book of Acts, Paul was imprisoned with Silas. Their feet and hands were bound, and they were placed in the inner cell. There was no way of escape. Their fate was in another's hands. Many soldiers would have lost hope. Joy and peace do not exist in dungeons where pain and anger run rampant. But Paul and Silas did not lose heart because they focused on God. They prayed and sang praises to Him.[24] Their response was not of the world, but of soldiers of Christ, who walked with the shoes of the preparation of the gospel of peace strapped to their feet. Like Theo and the messenger, they had no guarantee that they would live past the battle, but that did not stop them from fighting it. There was no guarantee Paul and Silas would be set free, but that did not stop them from trusting God, their firm foundation. Now God, according to His will, broke their chains and opened the doors in a miraculous way, something only God was able to do.[25] In the fiercest fight, He provides the ability to face the enemy. At our lowest points, He provides armor, a way through the battle, and a path to victory. In the moments of impossibility, He strengthens our souls and enables us to stand in His peace. Psalm 4:8 says, "I will both lie down in peace, and sleep; for You alone, O Lord, make me dwell in safety." When surrounded by the enemy, the common reaction is fear or anxiety, yet the psalmist says it is through the Lord that we can rest in peace.

## -Peace in God-

When we are going through difficult trials and hardships, we feel worn down, tired, and dirty. But we need to understand that the enemy cannot take our peace from us. He can throw filth at us and make the battle harder, but he does not hinder us. He cannot stop us. We can walk in peace.

Elijah was a prophet of God. He often stood against the evil in the land and proclaimed the truth. When faced with unequal odds, Elijah remained rooted with his feet in God's peace. The face-off on Mount Caramel to prove who the true God was encompassed one such battle. For hours, the prophets of Baal shouted and cut themselves trying to bring fire from heaven by the power of Baal. When Elijah prayed, God sent fire to consume his offering, proving Himself as the one true God.[26] Elijah was dedicated and stood firm on the side of God, and God showed His power. A victory had been won, but then the enemy continued to attack, throwing filth on him and trying to stop him from fighting. Following the miraculous victory on Mount Carmel and the fulfillment of rain in a three-year drought, Jezebel set out to kill Elijah.[27] In fear, he fled.[28] Frightened, weary, and desperate, he asked God to end his life.[29] Even the strongest soldiers encounter mudslides. But God, who knows all, sent an angel to strengthen him. There was more for Elijah to do for God.[30] The battles were not over.

As the messenger instructed Theo, the enemy will not stop. In the war we face, we are fighting for spiritual ground and souls. Yet, if we endure and remain steadfast through the fight, Christ grants us an inner, eternal, peace that lasts.

When we know what God has called us to do, there is a peace that we can claim as Theo did when he fearlessly took his stand. He knew it was not going to be easy, but he was determined to face it. Theo had God's peace within himself. We, too, can have that same peace. Christ tells us in John 14:27, "My peace I give to you." Paul tells the church at Colossae, "let the peace of God rule in your hearts, to which you also were called in one body; and be thankful."[31] There is a measure of God's peace that comes when we choose to be thankful. Spiritual and physical wars are dirty affairs, and as we fight and walk through them, mud and blood gather around and cover our feet. But if we trust and thank God with each step, He helps us to get through it all, with His peace.

# -Standing in Christ-

This strength and peace in the middle of the battle has to do with a placement of ourselves with God. When we grow tired during or after a battle, it is vital for us to draw near to God, thank Him for enabling us to fight and entrusting us with our spiritual castles. We ask Him to renew our strength. Elijah could not continue the required journey before him on his own strength. He needed God. The messenger told Theo, "When we try to do things in our own strength, that is when we fail. We must trust and stand in Him who is stronger than ourselves." God provided Elijah with what he needed. The King provided armor for Theo and sent the messenger to strengthen him. God does the same for us. He provides us with armor, sends us the Holy Spirit, and guides us through the battles. He strengthens us,[32] restores us, and gives peace to our souls.[33] He is the Rock on which we stand. As David says in the Psalms, "The Lord is my rock and my fortress and my deliverer; my God, my strength, in whom I will trust." [34] It is through the strength and peace of Christ that we can endure the battles. Are you ready? We prepare; we armor up and put on the shoes He has given us. We stand our ground and fight our King's enemy. The everlasting, eternal peace soldiers long for will come at the end of the war. We must not give up and surrender our peace to the enemy. We must stand firm. If we firmly plant our feet in God, like the soldier whose shoes had spikes to help hold his ground, we can stand and not be shaken. We stand in perfect peace as we stand in Christ Jesus. The war will rage. Nevertheless, we will not be fearful soldiers but prepared warriors who will not surrender, holding firmly to Christ. We know the truth–at the end of the war it will be through Christ that we gain eternal peace and victory.[35]

# The Shield of Faith

*"Above all, taking the shield of faith with which you will be able to quench all the fiery darts of the wicked one." - Ephesians 6:16*

The messenger equipped Theo with a shield of defense. Paul instructs us as soldiers to take up "the shield of faith," and with it we "will be able to quench all the fiery darts of the wicked one." The shield is a vital piece of armor. Unlike the pictures of small round shields like the Greeks used, historically, the Roman war shields stood about four feet tall and two feet wide–large enough to protect a man but not hinder him from walking with it. The protection the shield offered could be used in different ways. It was a covering before or above the soldiers as needed. In many battles, they were known to use their shields like ramps for others to climb on to reach higher ground. The shield could be used to protect one man or many. If several men were to stand side by side and hold their shields in front, it would create a wall. Those behind the wall would be protected. Some shields were covered in animal skins, which would then be soaked with water, drenching the skins before going into battle. This allowed protection against fiery arrows. The wet skins would quench the flames and allow the soldiers to continue moving forward. Keeping the shield before him, a soldier would be able to advance or hold his ground as needed and without fear.

## -Trust in God-

In the spiritual war we fight, our faith is like a shield. It aids and protects us against the arrows of the enemy. When the enemy sends arrows of doubt and fear, we trust that God goes before us, and we know that the enemy has no power over us. Nevertheless, that does not stop him from trying to gain authority over the armies of God. Satan will continue to fight, but our faith in God enables us to stand courageously when we face those battles. In the Psalms, God is described as "a shield to all who trust in Him."[1] He is our Protector in the fight. We must not fear. He goes before us.

Throughout the battle, the messenger told Theo not to be afraid. Fear brings doubt; trust brings courage. When we fear, our trust falters. We become like Theo when he shook and dropped his shield. The fighting is inevitable. It *will* happen. But we do not have to enter the battle afraid. Just as the King equipped Theo, God equips us. Yet just because He equips us does not mean we are invincible and will never encounter pain or danger. We will all encounter battles, and some will be dangerous and painful, but with the Lord before us we can prevail. With His armor secure around us, we can stand and fend off the enemies' attacks.

## -Standing Against Impossible Odds-

With the shield of Faith, we can press on, to endure beyond what is humanly possible. Theo and the messenger battled and withstood impossible odds–two men against an army. In scripture, there is a similar battle: two men against an army. Jonathan, the son of King Saul, and his armorbearer stood against a Philistine garrison, yet impossible odds do not stop God. The Israelites had no weapons to fight with.[2] Therefore, the enemy kept the Israelite people in a state of fear. Without physical swords or shields, how could they stand? But God is not limited to the physical. As

Jonathan and his armorbearer prepared to face the enemy, Jonathan told the young man, "Nothing restrains the Lord from saving by many or by few."[3] God was with Jonathan and his armorbearer that day and brought about a great victory through them. Because Jonathan put his faith in God, he was able to stand against a garrison, and Jonathan knew it was the Lord who delivered the enemy into their hands. No matter what enemies we face, our faith in God allows us to stand firm in impossible situations. It is God who brings the victory. It is our responsibility to stand and fight. When we fight for God and stand in the truth, there is no need to fear the armies of evil. We are fully equipped for the fight.

## -Side-By-Side Defense-

Having been fully equipped, we must now stand and fight. We do not need to fear the ones who come against us. The enemy cannot penetrate the armor of God. Nevertheless, he will attempt it, and he will rain down arrows of fire, but if we hold firmly to our faith in Christ Jesus, the foe cannot break through our defense. During Roman battles, the soldiers would stand side-by-side and create a wall with their shields. They could move as a unit and push through the enemy lines or they could create a barracks with their shields. The enemy would shoot arrows in attempts to stop the soldiers, but the Romans were trained in the way of warfare. They knew their shields were essential assets. Not only could they create a wall before them, but those behind them lifted their shields and created a roof. This protected the soldiers from front attacks and attacks from above. This concept of a shield about them is what God provides for us. Faith and trust in God enable us to stand against the coming arrows and attacks of the enemy. So often God sends us fellow soldiers to be another shield. Just as the messenger was able to lift his shield for Theo, we can guard each other and be that wall of defense against the enemy. Throughout scripture, we are given examples of spiritual soldiers who are sent on missions to strengthen, encourage, and build the kingdom. Many spiritual soldiers were sent out by twos, providing a system of protection. Jesus, when He sent out the seventy to go heal, preach the word, and cast out demons, sent them out two-by-two.[4] In the beginning of the book of Acts, we see Peter and John together teaching and healing.[5] In Paul's missionary journeys, he traveled with other men. The first time, he took Barnabas with him. The second time, Silas went with him.[6]

Many of Paul's letters include acknowledgement of other believers, soldiers, who have done well and encouraged others in the faith. He speaks of men like Timothy, Epaphroditus, and Philemon.[7] In his letter to the Corinthians, Paul tells us to "watch, stand fast in the faith, be brave, be strong.[8] It is crucial that we follow Paul's instructions. The enemy will rise against us when we are least expecting it. He will try to shake our faith. He will tell us we are not able to stand, and he will strike to weaken and kill us. We must fight against him. We must lift our shield of faith and quench his arrows. Our shield was created to intercept and block those attacks of the enemy. Let us employ our shields and take our stand. Remember that God has not given us a spirit of fear, but of power, love, and a sound mind.[9] So let us use what He has given us as we wrestle against the spiritual enemy and fight the battle before us. Peter says we are to resist the enemy and remain steadfast in the faith.[10]

## -Faith in God-

Faith that stands firm is faith that is placed in God, not in tangible aspects but in the Creator of heaven and earth. Having faith is not a tool to get what we want. It is so we learn to trust. Faith is trusting God even when we cannot see. When we hold the shield above or before us, we must trust that it will block the arrows. If we stick our head out to the side, we make ourselves a target, and we are not practicing our faith. The messenger told Theo to trust in the King who gave him the armor. Even though he could not see the King physically, the King was present through his messenger and protected him with the armor. He did not leave Theo alone. The armor God gives us is not seen. Faith is the substance of things hoped for, the evidence of things unseen.[11] Though some of the battles we face may be physical, the spiritual battles we encounter are all unseen by the human eye. They must be perceived spiritually. When everything is taken from you and all seems to be failing, the human eye perceives it as if all is lost. Yet, if we look at life through the spiritual lens, we can see that faith is what allows us to remain standing in those difficulties while we are in the middle of the fight. Faith is our guard when all seems lost–not faith that we will get it all back, but faith that God is good and in control. We trust in God and hold firmly to Him. We like to think that life would be so much better if we did not have to go through trials. But trials allow us to grow as soldiers. God uses hardships and battles to strengthen us, to teach us to trust in Him, and to fight the enemy. A soldier who has never been tried will never become victorious. There is no glory for those who do not fight. So let us hold firm to the faith and battle the foes that rise against us.

## -Equipped for a Reason-

God equips us with a shield for a reason, and He expects us to use it. The shield does not lift itself; we must lift it. We must choose to take the action. Scripture tells us to whom much is given, much is expected.[12] If a soldier drags his shield by his side, how will he protect himself from an attack? We have the responsibility to use what has been given to us and not let it lie on the ground. As soldiers, we are equipped with a shield to quench the arrows and counter the attacks of the enemy. As the Roman soldiers' shields were soaked in preparation for fiery arrows, we need to immerse ourselves in the living water, in Christ's words, and ask Him to soak us in the Holy Spirit, so that when the enemy attacks with darts and arrows of fire, we can quench them by the water of the Holy Spirit. The enemy will come from different directions, especially in the thick of the battle. We must be ready and aware. We must trust in God and act according to His direction. Have faith and He will get you through.

## -Increased Attacks-

However, when we use our shield, it causes the enemy to increase his attacks. He attempts to sneak around, lay traps, and ensnare us. Do not lose heart and do not drop your shield. The enemy is watching and waiting for your shield to drop. He wants you depressed, downcast, and without your faith. Then he can take you down. Once Theo's shield dropped, the enemy wasted no time aiming and shooting an arrow at him. The enemy saw the lack of protection and moved in. But God sends us His Holy Spirit to guide us through the fight, and He outfits us for war. God is a shield around you.[13] He is there with you. And if He can strengthen David's arm to bend a bow of bronze, then He can strengthen our arms to hold up His shield of faith.[14] We must be on our guard. Do not let your mind get sidetracked. Stay focused on Christ, have faith, and hold onto Him no matter what comes against you. Do not be unwise and think that the enemy will not shoot at you because of your faith and belief in God or because you are a Christian Satan will not come against you. In the book of Ephesians, Paul bluntly tells us that fiery darts will be shot as us. We will face attacks from the enemy. He came against Christ. Therefore, we ought not to be so arrogant as to think he will not come after us. He will come at us even harder because we are followers of Christ. The darkness hates the light, and Satan wars against the soldiers of God. Satan is going to search for the easiest way, the quickest way to take us down. Therefore, we need to be aware of our weak spots and any sins we are allowing ourselves to enjoy. The enemy looks for the weakest structure in our wall. When the devil tempted Christ, he went after the physical hunger of a physical man. The enemy sent a ploy to the door with Theo before attacking the wall, and when he did attack the wall, he went for the weakest bricks. An enemy will not breach the strong points of the castle because he knows we are prepared for him there and that is the hard way. Enemies attack where we are weak. They look for their advantage in the fight, making it easier for them and harder for us. But if we look to God and are obedient, His power is made strong and proven triumphant in our weakness.[15] Remember, He gives us strength for each day. Paul encouraged the church that when he suffered for Christ's sake, when he endured the spiritual fight, he took pleasure in standing firm, "for when I am weak, then I am strong."[16] This weakness does not mean we are incapable of fighting, or that we do nothing or cower, but that when we allow Christ to work in us in whichever way He sees fit, His strength is what sustains us. When we depend on God, He gives us the strength to fight the battles that lie ahead. He does not leave us or forsake us.[17]

## -God Strengthens-

God has been sustaining and strengthening soldiers for thousands of years. The book of Hebrews speaks of individuals who, by faith, "subdued kingdoms, worked righteousness, obtained promises, stopped the mouths of lions, quenched the violence of fire, escaped the edge of the sword, [and] out of weakness were made strong."[18] God does not keep His soldiers *from* the fight; He strengthens them to endure *through* the fight. It is our job to trust Him and have faith. He is over all the battles we face. In the book of Judges, the Lord sent an Angel to a man named Gideon. God chose Gideon to save the people of Israel from the Midianites.[19] Gideon called for volunteers and thirty-two thousand men gathered to him, but the Lord had a different plan. He selected three hundred of those men. The rest went home. The Lord told Gideon, by these "three hundred men . . . I will save you, and deliver the Midianites into your hand."[20] God wanted Gideon and the men to trust Him. It was not by number that He would save, but by His power. In contrast to the Israelites, the enemy was "as numerous as locusts; and their camels were without number, as the sand by the seashore."[21] When we face an enemy greater than ourselves, we must lean on and trust in God who is able to do above and beyond what we are able. As the messenger reminded Theo, we do not put our faith and trust in our own strength or power because "it is not enough." "We have to trust and stand in Him who is [greater] than ourselves." And when we trust in God, our faith is tested. Do not be caught off guard. Prepare yourself for battle. Our shield will be hit. The question is: will we drop it because of the pressure, or will we press on through the fight? It is "not by might nor by power, but by [the] Spirit" of God that we are able to fight and conquer.[22] And if we endure through the battles, we gain knowledge of a tried soldier, and our faith grows. When Gideon was about to face the Midianites, God directed him to the enemy camp where God confirmed His power and victory. He strengthened Gideon's faith. When we come out of a fight, we can look back and see the faithfulness of God, and that strengthens us for what lies ahead. There was no logical reason for Gideon and his men to win. They were the weaker ones, but because of their faith and obedience, God saved all of Israel. He turned the enemy against one another and brought about a great victory using the faith and obedience of Gideon and his men. Even though Gideon was afraid, he was obedient. Yet, notice how the Lord strengthened his hand, for the battle begins in the mind. God reminded Gideon that He was over the battle. Gideon worshiped God and entered the fight trusting in Him who saves.[23] Theo was afraid when he saw the enemy, but the messenger strengthened him and told him not to fear. We do not need to fear the enemy or what lies ahead, for remember, greater is He who is in us than he who is in the world.[24]

We must trust and not lose faith in God. With this focus, we can strengthen our arms and hold onto our shields and block the attacks. If we do not, we become like Theo when he became afraid, sidetracked, and concerned with the things around him. He took his focus off the fight. He loosened his grip on the shield, and it was struck down with the next attack, and he fell. If we let go of our shield of faith, we have nothing to shield us from the enemy. James says faith without works is dead.[25] A soldier who does not wear his armor or use his shield is soon dead. Without the aid of the messenger's shield, Theo would have died with that arrow.

## -Dropping our Shield-

When we lose faith, when we drop our shields, we often turn and flee, or we become paralyzed with fear. Theo experienced both. He froze when he saw the enemy advancing, and he also longed to flee the battle when it increased. But he conquered the fear by trusting in the one who equipped him for the fight. He chose to continue to fight the battle as a good soldier. Sadly, many are deceived by the enemy to lay down their defenses. The enemy reasons with them, saying that if they do not fight, they will not get hurt, like in the letter to Theo. That is a lie. As the messenger said to Theo, do not believe the enemy's lies. With his lies, the enemy either numbs his victims, turns them against one another, or lets them think they are secure until he destroys them. Some even turn and join the enemy lines. They listen to the lies of promises that will never come and are pulled away and ensnared. Remember the story the messenger told about the man who wanted riches? He listened to the false promises, joined their cause by opening the door, and at the end, the enemy turned on him and locked him away to die. The enemy uses twisted words, and as the messenger said, "if you live by his terms, you will not live but surely die." In scripture, Ananias and Sapphira, two believers in Christ, were deceived by the enemy.[26] They did not fight against him, and Satan filled their hearts.[27] He ensnared them into joining his cause with riches. They lied against the Holy Spirit, and their alliance and submission to the enemy led to their deaths. Paul speaks of fellow believers, soldiers, who abandoned the fight being deceived because they loved the things of this world, and he cautioned Timothy to hold fast to the truth.[28] Even Peter fell to the desire of self-preservation and denied Christ.[29] Nevertheless, unlike others who would not repent, Peter wept, picked himself back up, and returned to fight. When he was convicted, he had remorse, humbled himself before God, and joined the fight again. Though his shield fell, he did not delay in picking it back up and continuing the fight.

# -Continue the Fight-

The King of heaven has equipped us with armor for the fight. We do not need to be afraid to stand on the battlefield or to encounter the enemy. We place our faith in God, His Truth, and He guides us through. Psalm 119:114 says, "You [Lord] are my hiding place and my shield; I hope in Your word." God is our shield. Our hope is in Him. During the battle, we can see the danger, but we are to have faith in God. If we grow tired, or slip, or if the enemy hits beneath the shield, we keep holding on. We must continue. It is still possible to win the fight after being wounded. Do not give up. Paul tells Timothy, "I have kept the faith."[30] He did not drop his shield. Even though he endured beatings, imprisonments, stoning, shipwrecks, and betrayal, he never let go.[31] He held onto the shield and had faith in Christ to the very end. Do you believe God is a shield about you? Are you willing to trust Him through the fight? When we walk in obedience and trust God, there is victory. Psalm 3:3 says, "You, O Lord, are a shield for me, my glory and the One who lifts up my head." To lift the head is to refocus our eyes and minds, to take them off ourselves and place them on God. For us to stand firm and win this spiritual battle, we must focus on Christ. If we let our minds remain focused on us, we will lose the battle, but if we look to Christ, He strengthens us. When we stand, we will bring glory to Him. He is our glory. We do not stand in our own strength but in God's power and might. He lifts our heads so we may be strengthened, see His truth, and continue the fight. When our faith is strengthened, we can better defend ourselves and others, creating a wall of faith so the enemy cannot break through.

# The Helmet of Salvation

*"And take the helmet of salvation, and the sword of the Spirit, which is the word of God." - Ephesians 6:17*

In the story, the messenger equips Theo with a helmet. Verse seventeen instructs us as soldiers to "take the helmet of salvation." The Roman helmet protected the soldier by covering the top and sides of the head, along with a flap shielding the back of the neck. The front protected the forehead without blocking the view, allowing the soldier to watch his surroundings and see what lay before him. Spiritually, the helmet is to guard our mind and our thoughts. The mind is the battle ground for spiritual warfare. In the mind is where we decide to fight, choose to stand, and plan our course of action. It is where the fight begins. It is as the messenger told Theo: "You must mentally block out the voice of the enemy. He must not enter your mind, for if he does, he will cause you to stumble, leading to total destruction." If he remains rooted in your thoughts, the enemy will do whatever he can to distract your mind. As spiritual soldiers, we must guard our souls. To do that, we must listen to and follow God. We must choose to stand against the enemy and fight. Joshua told the people of Israel to "choose for yourselves this day whom you will serve."[1] It is a choice we all must make for ourselves. Each soldier determines who he is fighting for before the fight begins.

# -Guard Your Mind-

The enemy will try to get into our head. We must block him and force him out. 2 Corinthians 10:5 tells us to take "every thought into captivity to the obedience of Christ." It is our job to be aware of our thoughts and capture those that are not in accordance with God or do not bring Him glory, but after we capture the thoughts, we are to deliver them to the higher authority–Christ. If we were to capture these thoughts, keep them locked up, and not surrender them to God, then they still have a foothold in our mind and can talk to us and ensnare us. When we give our thoughts over to Christ, they are no longer ours to deal with. We are free of them. As Theo crumbled the enemy's note and threw it to the wind, so we surrender our thoughts to Christ and toss them out of our minds. However, be on guard. Satan has a habit of bringing up old thoughts in attempts to ensnare us again. We have to literally give them over to Christ. It may help to physically say, "I capture this thought and deliver it to the obedience of Christ. Be silent in Jesus' name." Do it repeatedly until it is surrendered and you are free of it, and then fill your mind with things of Christ: praises and thanksgiving, scripture, prayers, hymns, and spiritual praise songs. The importance of filling our minds with things of God is depicted in the book of Matthew. Jesus speaks of the enemy's approach to an unprotected mind: "he goes through dry places, seeking rest, and finds none. Then he says, 'I will return to my house from which I came.'"[2] The house represents our minds. The enemy is constantly trying to gain access. After we fight him off, he will return at another time to attempt to regain control. If the house remains clean but empty, when the enemy comes back and sees it is empty, he brings seven others more evil than himself and they all infiltrate the house.[3] To fight this infiltration, we must fill our minds with Christ. To accomplish that, we must "set [our] mind[s] on things above, not on things on the earth."[4] To set our minds on things on the earth, carnal things, is to make a way for the destruction of the castle. But to focus on Christ is to make way for life and victory. Things above are the things of Christ. He is the One on whom we are to focus. Remember the devil is trying to direct our thoughts away from God. When Peter became distracted and argued against what Jesus foretold about His death, Jesus rebuked him and said, "Get behind Me, Satan! For you are not mindful of the things of God, but the things of men."[5] Christ was not fighting Peter. He was teaching Peter how to fight the voice of the enemy, and how to recognize it. Christ rebuked the voice and thoughts of the enemy. He chose to keep His mind on the things of God, on things above.

## -Salvation Comes From God-

In spiritual battles, we need deliverance just as we do in physical battles. Our deliverance, our salvation, comes from God. He equipped us with the helmet of salvation so we would be able to fight the thoughts of the enemy, be reminded of Christ, and find salvation in victory over the enemy. God is the One who gets us through the fight. Scripture tells us that the "salvation of the righteous is from the Lord."[6] He is our salvation. Psalm 68:20 says, "Our God is the God of salvation; and to God the Lord belong escapes from death." God has equipped us with the armor to face the enemy, and He has brought us an escape from death. He brought us salvation. However, as soldiers in a war, we must protect our minds with the helmet of salvation so that we can be victorious in these battles. God brings salvation, but we must choose to listen, follow, and obey Him. As soldiers in the Lord's army, we must choose to listen only to our Commander. The messenger told Theo when he dressed him for battle that the helmet was to help him keep out the voice of the enemy. And that is what we are to do. We must fight against the voice of the enemy and not let him invade our minds.

## -Focus on the Voice of God-

Do not let the voice of the enemy drown out God's voice. You get to choose what voice you focus on. If we allow ourselves to focus on the shouts and taunts of the enemy, we will be led astray. We will be like the man who desired the gold and riches. We will let ourselves be deceived by our desires. Consequently, we will be wounded, captured, or worse. We must keep our minds focused on the spiritual battle. Scripture tells us that "we do not war according to the flesh."[7] Nor do we wrestle against flesh and blood.[8] The "weapons of our warfare are not carnal but mighty in God for pulling down strongholds, casting down arguments and every high thing that exalts itself against the knowledge of God, bringing every thought into captivity to the obedience of Christ, and being ready to punish all disobedience when your obedience is fulfilled."[9] We are to strike down the thoughts of the enemy and submit to the obedience of Christ. We are in spiritual warfare. Yet, often, we become distracted and give in to the desires of the flesh. We let our minds lose focus and wander. And at times, we become our own source of distraction by filling our minds with things of this world. This only makes the battle harder for us to fight. And we create more battles we must overcome along with the one we are already fighting. The enemy does not need any more fodder. Do not help him snare you by giving in to the desires of the flesh. He already knows what is common to man, and he will use it against us. Do not give him the footing in your mind by preparing the ground for him. We must take all thoughts captive to the obedience of Christ. The battle does not belong to the enemy. It does not belong to us. It belongs to God. Scripture says, "the battle is the Lord's,"[10] and "deliverance is of the Lord."[11] Our mind is the battleground. It is where the spiritual fight occurs. So let us keep it focused on God. The book of Psalms tells us, "The Lord is my light and my salvation; whom shall I fear? The Lord is the strength of my life; of whom shall I be afraid?"[12] Focus on the voice of the Lord and trust in Him.

## -Idols and Distractions-

If we let the enemy whisper under our helmet, we allow an army of enticements and fear into our minds, and it will distract us. Distractions get our eyes off Christ and place the focus on something else. The longer we focus and dwell on the distraction, the blinder we become to the schemes of the enemy, and the more prominent the distraction becomes in our lives. It will eventually consume our time and take priority in our lives. At this moment, it becomes an idol. An idol is defined as any person or thing regarded with blind admiration, adoration, or devotion. Idols are anything we place above God. Idols consume our energy. They are at the forefront of our minds. They fill us with self-focus, and they never truly satisfy. They are like a plague–slowly killing from the inside–poisoning the spirit little by little. The man with the room full of gold had his mind focused on his desire for wealth. The gold became an idol to him. He was devoted to gaining it. It enveloped his mind. He no longer cared for anyone or anything else. His desire gave birth to sin when he let the enemy in the gates, and that decision brought death. We must be careful what we fill our minds with, what we listen to, watch, read, desire, and spend our time doing. If we fill up with things of this world, it will weaken our minds and produce fodder for the enemy. However, if we do as God told the people of Israel, and have "no other gods before [Him],"[13] if we put God first, keep Him as our focus, fill ourselves with His word and listen to Him when He speaks, we will be victorious over the enemy and produce a harvest of righteousness that is pleasing to Him.

## -Listen and Obey-

Throughout the gospels of Matthew and Mark, we are told "he who has ears, let him hear."[14] We are supposed to be listening *for* God and *to* God.

He will speak to us and direct us through the fights. Amidst the chaos of the battles, we may not always hear Him, or hear Him clearly, but that does not mean He is not there. Scripture tells us, He will never leave us.[15] Even in the thickest part of the battle, even when you feel like you cannot hear Him, set your mind on things of God, and home in on Him. He is there. However, if we choose to ignore His direction and refuse to listen, we will be like the Israelites in Ezekiel 12:2, "a rebellious [people], which has eyes to see but does not see, and ears to hear but does not hear." The Israelites were God's chosen people. They were His soldiers, but a soldier can choose to obey or ignore orders. They were aware of their responsibilities, but they became rebellious and would not return to the Lord. Through Ezekiel, God warned the people of the consequences of rebellion and the coming captivity.[16] Nevertheless, they would not listen nor turn from their evil ways. They would not return to the Lord. They would not fight the thoughts of the enemy. The Israelites were deceived by their own desires, and they fought against Ezekiel and his message, but Ezekiel focused on God's voice and was obedient. Both received the consequences for their actions. Ezekiel obeyed the voice of the Lord and faced the consequences of the world, but his reward was with God. The Israelites ignored Ezekiel's warning and faced the consequences of God's punishment. It is important that we hear and heed God when He speaks. As soldiers, we must train ourselves to listen to God's voice and act on His direction.

Putting on the helmet needs to be a reminder to us that we are to have the mind of Christ. Romans and Philippians both tell us that, as the body of Christ, we are to be of one mind. Moreover, this one mind is not my mind, nor is it your mind, but it is the mind of Christ Jesus.[17] Christ was focused on the battle before Him and would not, did not, turn away from the Father's plan. Christ humbled Himself before God and became obedient to death, even death on the cross.[18] As a soldier in God's army, when we put on that helmet, we are to put on the mind of Christ. We are to humble ourselves under God, our Commander, and be obedient to

Him, even unto death. The messenger was obedient and willing to fight the battle, regardless of the peril and danger that lay ahead. As he told Theo, "No matter what happens, I choose to stand and follow my King." In the spiritual battle, we as soldiers need to have that same mindset if we are to win the fight. God sees the bigger picture. He is like a Commander in a war: He has a map before Him. He knows what the future holds. Right now, we cannot see the whole layout, but if we listen to our Commander and follow His voice, He will direct us through the battle. He will lead us in the right way.

In each battle we face, we must make the decision to guard our mind. If we do not listen to God but choose to walk in our own strength, we will cause devastation to ourselves and sometimes to others as well. It is in these moments of weakness that the enemy advances and takes ground we are supposed to guard. The loss of ground often occurs when we become self-focused and do not listen to our Commander. We lose focus, or we become afraid. In the story, Theo grew fearful when he saw the vast number of enemies, and if he had retreated, he would have surrendered precious ground, but the messenger called out to him, reminding him that they were able to stand and fight. Theo listened, reset his mind on the battle and his orders to guard and protect it, and he continued the fight. He conquered the battle in his mind and was then able to fight the enemy without distraction. When facing enemies, the Holy Spirit calls to us, encourages us, strengthens us, and reminds us God is in control. Nothing is impossible with God. He empowers us to stand, fight, and overcome. We do not need to fear.

## -Danger of Pride-

However, the enemy has an arsenal of schemes. If he cannot detour us by fear, he turns to pride. We can become overconfident in our own skill and start a fight too soon. When we become overconfident or self-focused, we either advance too far or we let the enemy in by thinking we can handle it. Scripture gives us an example of this in the book of Acts. The seven sons of Sceva thought they could take on the enemy (a demon) on their own. However, their focus was not on Christ but on themselves. They went in search of the enemy, and he came, but they were not prepared for the fight. They attempted to cast out a demon in the name of Paul's God. The demon replied, "Jesus I know, and Paul I know; but who are you?"[19] and with that he beat them and stripped them naked. They ran away defeated before the enemy. They entered the fight without being commanded to and fought in their own power, with a mind not set on Christ. In this spiritual battle, we are not to go looking for the enemy. We are to stand and be ready. And when Christ calls us to battle, we obey. In the book of Proverbs, it says the horse is prepared for battle, but victory belongs to the Lord.[20] We are to stand ready and be prepared. It is all about God's timing and plan. We are to be ready to go when He sounds the charge. He will win the victory over the enemy. And it will be done in His power, wisdom, and timing, not ours. We will be tempted to move before God calls, but we must resist temptations and remain standing where God places us. If the man with the army had stood fast and not compromised and surrendered to the enemy, he and his men would have lived. Perhaps they could have even overpowered the enemy and saved his family. But instead, he moved from his stand and thought to come to an agreement with the enemy. His mind was not focused on the battle, but on the pain. Unfortunately, the consequence of his actions, giving up his stance and ground, brought death to his men, family, and eventually himself. Moving when God has not called is detrimental to any soldier. Even if the path seems reasonable or looks like an easier route, do not lose focus. Keep the helmet secured. Keep your mind focused on Christ. Stand and trust God. He will tell us what to do, where to go, when to move, and how to complete the task. Will we listen and be obedient?

# -Christ Focused-

We want to be Christ-focused, Christ-centered, and Christ-minded. In Christ, there is life. Christ said, "I have come that [you] may have life, and that [you] may have it more abundantly."[21] Christ does not want us to perish.[22] He wants us to be victorious. To gain the victory, we need to keep Christ as our focus. One way to help ourselves is to find little things that trigger our thoughts and reset our minds on Him. The cross is a wonderful example of this. Every time we see a cross, we are reminded of Christ and His sacrifice. Philippians 4:8 encourages us to think on things that are true, noble, just, pure, lovely, of good report, anything virtuous, and anything praiseworthy. This list points to and reveals Christ. Christ said, "I am the way, the truth, and the life."[23] James refers to us as called after Christ's "noble name,"[24] a worthy name. The book of Acts speaks of Christ being the Just One.[25] John speaks of Christ as being pure.[26] Scripture says there is no greater love than for a man to lay down his life for a friend.[27] The Father so loved the world that He gave His only begotten Son to die for us.[28] God is love.[29] We have the good report of the Gospel of Jesus Christ, the salvation from sins and life eternal. We are called to be like Him and follow His virtuous example. Psalm 18:3 says, "I will call upon the Lord, who is worthy to be praised." When we reflect on Philippians 4:8, we reflect on Christ, His life and example.

Now, sometimes we will get distracted and fall. The devil will tell us that we have failed and are no longer able to fight, that he has the power. Do not listen to him. Tighten your helmet, and do not let the fall hinder you from getting back up, drawing near to God, and crying out to Him for deliverance and guidance. As the messenger said, "Do not focus on the evil of what could have been. That guilt is a tactic of the enemy to get your mind off the battle at hand... Let us learn from our mistakes and grow stronger." Throughout the book of Judges, the people of Israel lost their focus. They became sidetracked by the things of the world and the ploys of the enemy. They would fall, suffer the consequences, call out to God, repent, and once again set their mind on Him. He heard their cry, saw that they humbled themselves, and showed them mercy. He then brought salvation, delivering them from the enemy. This is not an excuse to keep sinning and wander away. Paul asks in his letter to the Romans, "Shall we continue in sin, that grace may abound? Certainly not!" [30] God forbid! This is a reason to get back up, to keep fighting. God knows the heart and sees if there is true repentance. David says, "the Lord searches all hearts and understands all the intent of the thoughts. If you seek Him, He will be found by you; but if you forsake Him, He will cast you off forever."[31] True repentance entails turning from your sin and walking the opposite direction. One day we will run out of time. One day the war will be over, and we will be judged according to where we are standing and who our minds are set on. Therefore, put on the helmet, stay focused on God, and let Him be your salvation and deliverance in the fight. Choose where your mind will be focused.

# The Sword of The Spirit

*"And take the helmet of salvation, and the sword of the Spirit, which is the word of God." - Ephesians 6:17*

As Theo removed the sword from the wall, he thought he was ready, but there was much to learn about the weapon he held and the technique needed to fight. As soldiers, we are instructed to take the sword of the Spirit, which is the word of God. According to the Greek, the word used here for sword refers to a large knife. This is not the type of broadsword knights would carry or a fencing sword, but rather it is a long dagger meant for close-range and hand-to-hand combat. There are times in battle when the enemy is not content with shooting arrows, so he comes into our territory. In those moments, hand-to-hand combat is required. Theo's responsibility was to guard the castle, to stand, and to fight. While the enemy was outside the walls, he was able to defend with bow and arrow. But once the enemy broke through and advanced against him, he had to fight hand-to-hand combat. In historical times, hand-to-hand combat is paralleled with wrestling. When two men wrestle, they grab each other with the goal of getting the opponent on the ground. Satan aims to knock us down. He wants to defeat us. His purpose is to destroy us.

# -Determination to Fight-

In the Roman Olympic Games, in the sport of wrestling, the winner received a crown with his victory. The loser had his eyes gouged out. This consequence created a necessity to win, a sense of urgency and a mindset for battle. When we view our spiritual battles with a mindset of life or death, the importance of victory increases. No longer is it an imaginary battle, but it is real, and life is at stake. When Theo made the final decision to fight, he knew what was at stake, and he knew he would have to fight to the end before victory was assured. As Christian soldiers, we need to demonstrate that same dedication. That determination will grow in us the desire, the urge, to fight and win the battle. Victory comes after the war. If we do not fight against Satan, we will become spiritually blinded, and he can defeat us without trouble. A spiritually blind soldier is unaware and easily overpowered. When we encounter the enemy in hand-to-hand combat, we must fight him. If we do not battle the enemy, he will destroy us. If we ignore him, we will be trampled by him. If we are not prepared, we will suffer from the attack. We must stand and fight the enemy, and no matter how many times we stumble or are knocked down, we get back up, stand strong, and keep fighting. When Theo fell, the messenger told him to get up and not be afraid. He said, "we are fully equipped" to fight the enemy. In his ministry, Paul suffered attacks from those who did not believe and who sought to silence the teaching of God's word. Throughout the book of Acts, trials and battles arose from those whose goal was to kill Paul. These opponents pursued Paul from Antioch, to Iconium, to Lystra until they finally persuaded the multitudes and "stoned Paul and dragged him out of the city, supposing him to be dead."[1] However, though he was struck down, Paul was not destroyed. Luke records that "he rose up and went [back] into the city."[2] Nothing would keep Paul from continuing the fight. Though the enemy knocked him down, he rose up again.

# -Be Aware-

Our sword allows us to defend ourselves against the enemy. But to stay fully prepared, we need to be aware. During the fight, soldiers must be alert and discerning of their surroundings. When the Lord called Gideon to fight for the deliverance of His people, God chose the men who were aware of their surroundings to be those to fight the battle. In the testing to see who would fight, God tells Gideon to separate those who drank water by getting down on their knees to drink from those who brought the water to their mouths.[3] After Gideon had separated the men into the two groups, "the Lord said to Gideon, 'By the three hundred men who lapped I will save you, and deliver the Midianites into your hand. Let all the other people go, every man to his place.'"[4] The three hundred who lapped brought the water up to them. This method would allow them to keep watch over their surroundings. Those who put their face in the water were not called to the battle. They were not cautious of their surroundings. They would not have been able to see an enemy approaching if their faces were in the water. The dangers of the lack of awareness of their surroundings could cost them their lives. Therefore, by the three hundred who were aware and watchful, God brought victory. We must always be on our guard. Whether in the thick of the battle or in the calm of our own castle, we are to be on watch and stay aware. When the fighting was at a pause, Theo and the messenger took turns standing watch. Yet, when Theo let his guard down and fell asleep, the enemy snuck in and attacked. The enemy waits for opportunities when our guard is down to strike us. We must, therefore, as the messenger said, "stay alert. Never let your guard down." The enemy will come when we least expect him. His thrusts will be quick, and he will aim to kill. Jesus told his followers, the enemy comes "to steal, and to kill, and to destroy."[5] We must be aware and be watchful soldiers.

# -Be Discerning-

In addition to being watchful, we are to be discerning. We are to discern what we encounter, to test it, and see if it comes from God. The enemy attempts to cause us to let down our guard, to let him in without a fight like the stranger did to Theo. But we are to discern, to know the difference between the things of God and the things of the enemy. It is not just about physical appearance but the intent. When the stranger came to the castle door, Theo was going to let him enter. He appeared innocent and in need. But the messenger stopped him saying, "We cannot let just anyone into the castle," everyone, everything, must be tested. John says we are to test the spirits, to discern and know whether they are from God.[6] The messenger and Theo tested the intruder with time and soon discovered his true intentions. The enemy sends spies to our castles all the time. We must be careful and discerning of spiritual matters, to know and recognize the ploys of the enemy. To do that, we are to seek God's wisdom, search His word, and listen for His commands on how to proceed.

In the book of Joshua, shortly after the victory over Jericho and Ai, the Israelites encountered a hidden enemy. Some men came deceptively from Gibeon. Like the spy at the castle, they dressed as if they were from a far country and said they were in search of Israel because of what God had done.[7] In reality, these men wanted to deceive Israel into an agreement not to attack their city. Joshua questioned them but did not stop to ask God for counsel on what to do. He tested the physical, but he did not test the spirit. In so doing, he let an enemy through the door. A short time later, the truth came out: he had been deceived. As soldiers, it is vital that we seek and ask God for counsel and wisdom before we act. He knows the thoughts, minds, and intents of the heart. He sees beyond the outward appearance. In 1 Samuel 16:7 the Lord tells His soldier Samuel, "Do not look at his appearance or at his physical stature, because I have refused him. For the Lord does not see as man sees; for man looks at the outward appearance, but the Lord looks at the heart." The book of Proverbs says, "the Lord weighs the spirits,"[8] and it is He "who weighs the hearts."[9] In the book of Jeremiah, God is referred to as the One who searches the heart.[10] In the letter to the Hebrews, He is a discerner of thoughts.[11] In the letter to the Thessalonians, we learn that it is "God who tests our hearts."[12] And in the book of Revelation, it says, "I [God] am He who searches the minds and hearts."[13] We are in a spiritual war. We cannot prevail over Satan if our mindset remains on the physical. We must look at the spiritual. To see the spiritual clearly, we must focus on God and let Him reveal the truth to us as He did to Samuel. Scripture warns us that the heart of man is deceitful.[14] Therefore, we are not to believe whatever comes knocking at the door of our hearts and minds, our castles, but we are to test everything. There are evil spirits, and Satan will send spies as deceptions to cause us to believe he is an ally. Be cautious; he is an expert in hiding the truth. Scripture tells us that the devil transforms himself into an angel of light.[15] It is one way he deceives people. Just like the enemy spy dressed up in beggar clothes, our enemy puts on a façade, a disguise of deception. He is the deceiver,[16] a murderer, and the father of lies.[17] Therefore, we must pray, seek godly counsel, and listen for God to show us the truth through spiritual discernment.

It is vital to test the spirits we encounter. Are they of God? Or are they distracting us from God? Anything that distracts our minds from God or that does not point us to God should not be let into our castles. They will not strengthen us in the fight or help us stand against the enemy. So, how do we stop these intruders from entering? We fight them. We stop them where they are and do not let them take root or gain entrance into our castles. We tell our minds "No, I will not think on that." We turn them away. Not in our own power or words, but we fight the enemy with God's sword, His word. The letter to the Hebrews tells us that "The word of God is living and powerful, and sharper than any two-edged sword."[18] The enemy has no power against God. He has no ground to stand on, and in the end, he will surrender to Christ. As the messenger informed Theo, the enemy will be conquered when the King comes. Yet, in this life, we must stand firm, fight, and stay in tune with God in order to combat with accuracy and power. For when we stand in God, "no weapon formed against [us] shall prosper."[19] And as the messenger encouraged Theo, we also have been given the weapons needed to fight the enemy.

## -Fight-

The enemy cannot stand against God's power, and he knows it. But if he can deceive us into fighting in our own strength, he will be able to take us down. When he tempted Christ in the wilderness, he laid physical traps, trying to make Him focus on the physical and not the spiritual. But Jesus fought with God's word against the enemy. He fought the spiritual battle along with the physical temptations. He struck down Satan's ploys and pierced through the façade, stood His ground, fought back, and Satan left. "It is written" was His countermove to Satan's attacks. He used God's word and sword against the enemy. We, too, can fight the enemy as Christ did. Scripture says, greater is He who is in us than he who is in the world,[20] and it is Christ who lives in us.[21] If Christ resides in us, nothing is impossible. In John 14, Christ told the disciples, "He who believes in Me, the works that I do he will do also; and greater works than these he will do. . . ."[22] As Christ stood against the enemy, we can stand against the unseen adversary and prevail. We are not unaware of the enemy's schemes. We have been given the sword of the Spirit to combat spiritual darkness. When Satan attacks, let God's sword, His word, be your weapon of defense. In the letter of James, we are told to submit to God, to resist the devil, and to draw near to God. When we do that, the enemy must flee.[23] When we stand and fight using the sword of the Lord, we do not stand in vain, for the word of the Lord does not come back void. As He says through the prophet Isaiah, the word that goes forth from His mouth shall not return to Him void, "but it shall accomplish what [He] please[s], and it shall prosper in the thing for which [He] sent it."[24] God sent us His Spirit and His sword so that we are able to accomplish what He has given us to do: fight and prevail over the enemy. When we fight the enemy with God's word, we will overcome. It may not be immediate. Some skirmishes are quickly won, like the enemy who choked Theo in the night. The messenger overcame him in a moment. Other battles take time, dedication, persistence, and patience. As the messenger told Theo, we do not know when it will be over, but we fight with every breath. If we do not give up but continue to fight against the schemes of the devil, we will be victorious.

Do not be afraid to enter the fight or to use the sword God has given you. He has equipped us for battle. He prepares us for the fights. When God called Moses to go to Egypt, He told him, "I have surely seen the oppression of My people who are in Egypt . . . I know their sorrows. So I have come down to deliver them out of the hand of the Egyptians . . ., and I will send you."[25] Moses argued that he was not the man to do this, but God had already prepared him for this task. Every obstacle that Moses saw, God overcame. He informed Moses that He would be with him.[26] He would send Aaron as a spokesman; He would put the words needed in Moses' mouth, and He would teach him what to do.[27] The Lord does the same for us. God has already prepared us for the fight against the enemy. He sent us the Holy Spirit to guide and speak with us. He has put the sword of the Spirit, His word, in our hand, and He teaches us how to fight evil, deliver the oppressed, and overcome. If we ask Him, God will show us how to use it accordingly. When Moses doubted his orders and expressed his concern, the Lord asked him, "What is that in your hand?" Moses replied, "A rod."[28] From that moment, God opened Moses' eyes. He told him, "You shall take this rod in your hand, with which you shall do the signs."[29] In the battle against Pharaoh and the Egyptians, God wielded a rod of power. He spoke the word, the rod struck, and the fight ensued. The weapon God gave to Moses was already in his hand. He just needed to wield it. God demonstrated the might of His word to Moses as a reinforcement of His power. The sword of the Spirit is God's weapon for us to take down strongholds and overcome the enemy. So, let us not doubt, or fear, or flee at persecution, but let us rise up to the occasion, answer God's call, and take up the sword of the Spirit that He has already put in our hands.

As Theo was prepared for battle, the Lord prepares us for war. He has raised a chosen generation, an army of warriors. He calls us His own people.[30] He enlists us as soldiers.[31] And He empowers us with the sword of His Spirit, the word of God, just like the King of the Highlands did for Theo. The battle is upon us, and we are called to fight. So, pick up your sword and get ready. The day of the Lord is coming, and in that time His army will arise "like a strong people set in battle array."[32] God is our commander, and "the Lord gives voice before His army, for His camp is very great; for strong is the One who executes His word."[33] Those who encountered the angelic warriors who were sent to execute the word of the Lord experienced a holy fear and fell before them. To Joshua, God sent the Commander of His heavenly army, described as having "His sword drawn in His hand."[34] Joshua, fell on his face to the earth when he heard the Angel say, "as Commander of the army of the Lord I have now come."[35] Then the Lord gave His orders to Joshua of how to proceed with the coming battle against Jericho. Balaam also experienced the angelic forces of the Lord's heavenly army. When Balaam acted in disobedience, the Lord sent His angel to strike him. Yet, "the Lord opened Balaam's eyes, and he saw the Angel of the Lord standing in the way with His drawn sword in His hand; and [Balaam] bowed his head and fell flat on his face."[36] David also, when he had done wrong, "lifted his eyes and saw the angel of the Lord standing between earth and heaven, having in his hand a drawn sword,"[37] and David fell to his face in repentance, for "he was afraid of the sword of the angel of the Lord."[38] And God had mercy on him. Those who encountered God's sword, whether for or against them, saw the magnitude of God's power. When we wield God's sword, it has the power to strike the enemy, it is sharper than any two-edged sword. It can pierce through anything. If we are on the Lord's side, this sword brings power and victory, yet, if we turn against God, this sword brings judgment and destruction on those who are disobedient.

Therefore, let us stand strong in battle array and execute our orders with courage. The Lord told Joel to proclaim to the people, "Prepare for war! Wake up the mighty men, let all the men of war draw near, let them come up."[39] It is time to rise up for battle, and as the soldiers with Gideon proclaimed, let us also declare power for "the sword of the Lord!"[40] It was the sword of the Lord that they fought with, and it was the Lord Who brought victory over the impossible enemy, turning the enemy's own swords against themselves. It is as the Lord told the people of Israel, "Happy are you, O Israel! Who is like you, a people saved by the Lord, the shield of your help and the sword of your majesty! Your enemies shall submit to you, and you shall tread down their high places."[41] We will have victory over the enemy if we stand in the power of God's might and with His sword drawn in our hand.

## -Swords Ready-

In order for us to gain the victory over the enemy, however, our swords must be ready in our hands. It will do us no good in a struggle if we leave it sheathed. The heavenly warriors God sent to enact His orders each had their sword drawn and ready. When the messenger saved Theo from the enemy who was trying to kill him in the night, he used his sword and pierced the enemy between his armor. The messenger was ready for an attack, and his sword was in his hand. We need to be able to act just as quickly as the messenger. God has given us His Spirit and His word, and we need to be ready. The scriptures are filled with God's spoken words to His soldiers. They are a guide for us along with the Holy Spirit. When the enemy comes and attacks, we are to respond as Christ did, speaking the words of God.[42] But to know God's words, we need to spend time with Him and study the scriptures He has left for us. Theo did not know how to use his sword until the messenger instructed him how to fight. We will not know how to use our swords until we gain understanding and knowledge and direction of the Holy One. Because we cannot just have knowledge of the sword, we must have contact with the sword. We must live each day with the sword in our hand and the word in our hearts. As God instructed the Israelites, we also are instructed, "the word is very near you, in your mouth and in your heart, that you may do it."[43] We are to keep our swords near us and God's word in us at all times, for to be a true soldier of God, we need to know the words of God so that we are able to execute His orders in the battle.

In Paul's letter to the Ephesians, when describing the sword of the Spirit, the word of God, He uses "rēma" which is the Greek term for the spoken word. God's words are alive, they are breathed. Paul tells Timothy, "All Scripture is given by inspiration of God, and is profitable . . . for instruction in righteousness, that the man of God may be complete, thoroughly equipped for every good work."[44] In the Greek, it literally means it is God-breathed. God has not stopped breathing. He has not stopped instructing His soldiers how to fight. Sometimes He uses the written word, and sometimes He uses the spoken word. For the soldiers of the Old Testament, there was not a written word available to them as we have in the Bible today. They had God's words which He spoke to them, and through His words they fought the enemy and won the battles. Gideon was working when the Angel of the Lord came and spoke God's instructions to him.[45] Noah, "being divinely warned of things not yet seen . . . prepared an ark for the saving of his household."[46] He did not let the voice of the enemy overcome him. He fought using the truth of God's word, for God had spoken to him and given him his orders, and Noah obeyed. There is a list of individuals in Hebrews whom God led through battles and in victory by His spoken word. Those who "quenched the violence of fire, escaped the edge of the sword, out of weakness were made strong, became valiant in battle, turned to flight the armies of the [enemies]."[47] God has never stopped empowering His soldiers though the sword of the Spirit. He is not limited to the past, but He is the same yesterday, today, and forever.[48] As Christ told the disciples, the Holy Spirit "will teach you all things, and bring to your remembrance all things that I said to you."[49] The Holy Spirit is Christ's Messenger to us to teach us how to fight. As the King sent the messenger to Theo, God sends the Holy Spirit to us. And we are to accept, listen, and obey His commands. We are to be like the apostles, ready and willing to do whatever He calls us to do, whenever He calls us. There will be times when the battles around us are so deep that in the struggle we do not have time to sit back and decipher how to counter the enemy's attack. When Theo was knocked to the ground and an opponent stood over him with a sword coming down, Theo had to act quickly. We, too, must act swiftly. We employ the power of the sword of the Spirit, and in those moments, it is the Holy Spirit who guides our swords. He is the One who pierces through the enemy's armor and his lies. We do not need to fear, for Christ told them, "Do not worry beforehand.... But whatever is given you in that hour, speak that; for it is not you who speak, but the Holy Spirit."[50] The Holy Spirit will bring to your mind the truth of God's word. He will direct and lead you in the path of righteousness. But we must know Him and be familiar with God's voice and words. The word of God strengthens our hands and directs the dagger into the heart of the matter. As Christ spoke the word of God in the desert temptations, when we speak the words of God against the enemy, the truth cuts through the lies, "for the word of God is living and powerful, and sharper than any two-edged sword, piercing even to the division of soul and spirit, and of joints and marrow, and is a discerner of the thoughts and intents of the heart."[51] The word of God is living and active. He pierces the lies of the enemy, reveals the truth, and brings salvation. He will bring the victory; we must simply fight and obey.

# -Overcoming Evil-

We must counter evil with good. Paul says, "Do not be overcome by evil, but overcome evil with good."[52] When the lies arise, we speak truth. When darkness invades, we are to shine the light. When the enemy throws false accusations and guilt at us, we rebuke him in the Name of the Lord. In Jude, we find the archangel Michael and the devil in a verbal battle, and Michael says, "The Lord rebuke you!"[53] Michael knew Who held the power and Who had the authority. In Zechariah's vision of the high priest, he stands before the Angel of the Lord and Satan stands to oppose him, and at the attacks and accusations, "the Lord said to Satan, 'The Lord rebuke you, Satan!'"[54] We are to rebuke the devil in Jesus' name. But only soldiers of Christ can overcome the enemy in this way. In the book of Acts, we find men who were not obedient soldiers of Christ attempting to use the same authority to cast out a demon in the name of Paul's God, "and the evil spirit answered and said, 'Jesus I know, and Paul I know; but who are you?'" and he "overpowered them, and prevailed against them."[55] To overcome the enemy, we must be in unity with the One who has all power and authority, and we must keep His sword in our hand. Jesus told his disciples, "These signs will follow those who believe: In My name they will cast out demons . . . ."[56] The apostles healed and cast out demons in the name of Jesus. On one occasion, a girl with a spirit of the devil in her followed Paul and Silas in attempts to draw away those who heard the words of God: "Paul, greatly annoyed, turned and said to the spirit, 'I command you in the name of Jesus Christ to come out of her.' And he came out that very hour."[57] It was not in Paul's power that the enemy was overcome, but it was through the power of God. As the book of Revelation tells us, those who overcame the accuser "overcame him by the blood of the Lamb and by the word of their testimony, and they did not love their lives to the death."[58] As soldiers of God, we are to overcome the enemy through Jesus Christ and with the

Sword of the Spirit, the word of God. And as we overcome, our testimony glorifies God. Is your testimony glorifying God? The messenger reminded Theo that he had been given wisdom, power, and authority, a strength that none could truly comprehend. And that power and strength enabled him to fight a battle that seemed impossible to win. The battles we face and the enemy we encounter may seem impossible to us, but God has given us power and authority to overcome, and we will overcome through His name.

# -Take Heart-

Nevertheless, power over the enemy and our position in the fight does not stop the enemy from advancing against us. The enemy knew the castle belonged to the King of the Highlands, but that did not stop him from attacking it. Satan knew Jesus was the Christ, the Son of God, but that did not stop him from tempting and attacking Him.[59] The enemy knows that his demise is coming, that he will no longer prevail when the King comes. He will be cast into the bottomless pit.[60] Yet, until that time, the enemy camps around our castles and makes war against the soldiers of God. We must take heart, and do as David says, "though an army may encamp against me, my heart shall not fear; though war may rise against me, in [God] I will be confident.... I would have lost heart, unless I had believed that I would see the goodness of the Lord in the land of the living."[61] Everything God does and the things He allows are for good reason and are turned for good. Paul tells us in his letter to the Romans that "all things work together for good for those who love God, to those who are called according to His purpose."[62] This does not mean all things are easy, or pleasant, or happy. It means God has called us to be soldiers, and He works everything for good. While waiting for reinforcements from the King to come, Theo learned how to stand against the enemy, how to defend the castle, how to fight, and how to endure. He did not consider this good at the time, for he did not wish to fight at all. However, he learned that it was for his good. It was to help him fight the enemy and overcome. The good that God does through our battles may not feel good, but it is strengthening us and teaching us how to be better soldiers for Christ. The war may seem bleak and hopeless. At times, we may feel like Theo and wonder, "How long?" Yet, our timetable is not God's timetable. Scripture tells us, "The Lord is not slack concerning His promise, as some count slackness,"[63] but He is patient,[64] and at the right time He will come[65] and the enemy will be destroyed.[66] In the book of Second Chronicles, King Jehoshaphat and the people of Judah gathered to ask the Lord for guidance and deliverance from their enemies. Jehoshaphat knew that he was not able to conquer this enemy in his own power, but he knew Who was able to save them. Jehoshaphat cried out to God, "we have no power against this great multitude that is coming against us; nor do we know what to do, but our eyes are upon You."[67] We have no power against the enemy, but God has equipped us with His power so we can stand and fight. The messenger told Theo, even though the King is not physically here, He is still protecting us, and it is His sword we fight with. It is the Lord who brings salvation. When we do not know what to do, we turn to God and ask Him to teach us. God guides us in the battle, and if God is for us, then who can be against us[68] when we fight with His sword in our hand?

# Praying Always

*"Praying always with all prayer and supplication in the Spirit, being watchful to this end with all perseverance and supplication for all the saints."*
*- Ephesians 6:18*

The messenger equipped Theo with the required armor and sword, but he also equipped him with the weapon of a bow and arrows. Jesus told the people at the temple, "It is written, 'My house is a house of prayer.'"[1] Our spiritual house, our castle, is a place for prayer. And the weapon of prayer has been given to us. After equipping us with armor and a sword, Paul reveals the weapon of prayer. He emphasizes the importance of prayer in stating that we are to pray always. This weapon of prayer is fourfold: We are to pray; we are to make supplications; we are to be watchful; and we are to persevere. After dressing Theo for battle, the messenger grabbed their bows and arrows. He told Theo, "Each battle calls for its own weapon. If you are unsure what that weapon should be, this is always a good one to start with." Prayer should be how we start every battle we face. Whether the enemy comes in with a full-on attack or attempts to invade, prayer is our first weapon of defense. Some enemies will never reach the wall due to the power of the arrows of prayer. This weapon of prayer is not just a child's bedtime prayer. This is a weapon of war, something we are to fight with.

## -Prayer an Effective Weapon-

Prayer is like the bow and arrows. It allows us to reach beyond ourselves. James tells us that the weapon of prayer is powerful and effective.[2] When the messenger entrusted Theo with the bow and quiver of arrows, he informed Theo of the power and effectiveness of such a weapon when used properly. We have been equipped with this weapon of prayer, and God expects us to use it responsibly and appropriately. Prayer is a powerful weapon in this spiritual war against the enemy. However, for it to be most effective will depend on our aim and how we stand. When Theo practiced with the bow and arrow, the messenger instructed him on the position of his posture and stance. Theo needed to align himself properly to hit the target. When we pray, we are to align ourselves with God. We bring Him our prayers and supplications, but we are to do so in an attitude of humility. Scripture says, "God resists the proud, but gives grace to the humble."[3] Jesus shared with His disciples the importance of being in the right spirit before God. When you go before God and you remember that your brother has an offense against you, do what you can to make it right with him and also within yourself, then come back and lay your gift or request before God.[4] It is important to be aligned with God so that when we pray, we shoot our arrows accurately, that they not go astray but hit the target. Scripture tells us the Lord hears the cry–the prayer–of the righteous, but He is far from the wicked.[5] And those who turn away from God, even their prayer is an abomination.[6] If we are standing rightly before God, then our weapon of prayer will be powerful and effective. But if we stray, our arrows of prayer will stray as well, and we will miss the mark. However, if we reposition ourselves and humble ourselves as Theo did, then the next time we release a prayer, we will hit much closer on the target. As we draw closer to God, He helps us to see clearly the enemies before us, and He strengthens our arms so that we do not grow weary in the battle. As the messenger encouraged Theo when his arms grew tired, God does the same for us. And the closer we are to God, the more accurately our weapon of prayer will be. Because when we humble ourselves, we no longer focus on ourselves but our focus is on God, and when we pray in accordance with His will, we hit the target.

# -Prepared for Battle-

Solomon says in the book of Ecclesiastes that there is "a time of war, and a time of peace."[7] As long as the enemy is fighting against the soldiers of Christ, we are in a time of war. Even though we may have times of relief, a soldier is to be constantly prepared for battle. Paul instructs Timothy that we are to be ready in season and out of season.[8] We are to be prepared for battle at any time. The enemy attacks whether we are ready for him or not. However, God equips us with armor and weapons so that we can always be ready for when the enemy attacks.

# -Be Watchful-

In Ephesians 6:18, Paul also mentions "being watchful to this end with all perseverance and supplication for all the saints." We must stay alert. The messenger cautioned Theo, "in the midst of a battle is not the time for rest or sleep but for action." Nevertheless, being overcome by exhaustion, Theo succumbed to the desire for sleep and closed his eyes while on watch. It was at that time the enemy infiltrated and attacked–not with a full force attack, but silently and subtly. We must be alert and watchful. Our adversary the devil lurks around seeking those whom he can devour.[9] And when we close our eyes to the spiritual fight, the enemy slips right in past our guard. Jesus told Peter, James, and John to stay ready and watch with Him in the garden.[10] They fell asleep. Christ woke them, saying, "Watch and pray, lest you [fall] into temptation. The spirit indeed is willing, but the flesh is weak."[11] Yet, they succumbed again to the desire of the flesh and fell asleep. It was that night the enemy returned to fight. In this attack, the temptations were not aimed at Christ alone but also at His disciples. Unlike the temptations in the desert, the disciples fell, for they were not ready. They were not being watchful. They were asleep and oblivious to the dangers encamping around them. To be ready for enemy attacks, we must be watchful and prayerful: watchful that we do not fall prey to the things of the world and prayerful that we do not fall asleep to the things of the Spirit.

## -Pray and Make Supplications-

Prayer is not just for us. Paul instructs us to pray and make supplication "for all the saints," our brothers and sisters in Christ. A good soldier does not only look out for himself but for others as well. The messenger did not just watch and fight for himself, but he also stood watch over Theo. We, too, are to watch out for others. When we see danger, we can lift our shield, draw our bow, or wield our sword as the fight demands. The battle we face, the war that rages, is not just against us individually. The enemy wants to demolish all of God's soldiers. In the book of Daniel, when King Nebuchadnezzar requires the wise men to tell him his dream and the interpretation, they say no one can do such a thing.[12] The king became angry and ordered that all the wise men be killed. Daniel was unaware of the king's decree until the guard came to carry out the orders. Daniel went to the king and "asked the king to give him time, that he might tell the king the interpretation."[13] It was not just Daniel's life at stake, but all the wise men were in danger, including his fellow soldiers Shadrach, Meshach, and Abednego. So, Daniel prayed; they all did. They sought "mercies from the God of heaven concerning this secret, so that Daniel and his companions might not perish with the rest of the wise men of Babylon."[14] God answered their prayer and gave Daniel the dream and interpretation so that he and those with him might live. Prayer is used not only to protect ourselves but others as well.

John, while exiled on the Island of Patmos, was instructed by God, "What you see, write in a book and send it to the seven churches."[15] He could see the battles ahead for the churches. And it was John's orders to warn them and prepare them. To each church, John writes "he who has an ear, let him hear."[16] He is sending messages of warning to help prepare and defend his fellow soldiers. He gives them encouragement on how to fight what is coming and what to be aware of. His vantage point of seeing the battle ahead is like that of an archer on the wall or in the watchtower. When Theo and the messenger stood in the watchtower, they could see the enemy approaching and release arrows at the foe. Once they were on the ground, the distance between them and the enemy decreased, and soon after they had to fight hand-to-hand combat. The revelation, given to John, is like a watchman for the seven churches. He stands in the tower, shooting at oncoming foes and warning those in the courtyard of what is coming. In this war, we are all under attack. At times, we are called to fight from the watchtower. At times, we fight beside each other. Prayer is a weapon that is used in every situation. Along with defending from the watchtower, the arrows of prayer are used to defend wounded soldiers. After Theo fell and narrowly escaped an attack from an enemy archer, the messenger drew his bow and struck the enemy, defending his fellow comrade. There will be times in our lives when we see others in need of spiritual backup. Do not be afraid to draw your bow or give a hand. Through prayer, God has equipped us to fight beside fellow soldiers in their times of need, just like the messenger was there to help Theo in his time of need.

## -Persevere in Prayer-

Paul instructs the soldiers to pray always. We are not finished fighting after one or two skirmishes. We are to persevere. We fight to the end. The war in the heavens is ever present, ever pressing, and we must be ever ready. The enemy will not be vanquished until the end. So, for now, the enemy surrounds the castle. He is looking for a way in. He attacks our walls and sends spies to our doors. Therefore, we must always be at the ready. We cannot let our guard down. We must be watchful, and we must persevere to the end. During Christ's battle in Gethsemane, He admonished His disciples to watch and pray.[17] Are we watching and praying? The fight is not over. As the messenger told Theo, the war is not over until the King returns, and "when the King comes . . . he shall smite the foes, and they will kneel or die before him." But until that time comes, we are to defend our castle with the weapon of prayer. We are to assist our fellow soldiers, to be watchful of the temptations, dangers, and enemies around, and to endure until the end. Paul says to be watchful. We need to be aware of our surroundings. We need to pray always. We must not stop fighting. The enemy wants you to give up your position. He wants you to surrender. But that cost is too high. We cannot afford to stop fighting. Our lives and the lives of others depend on our dedication to the fight. We are to persevere to the end and make supplication for all the saints. We must press on and endure. The fight is not against us alone, but all the soldiers of God. Therefore, we must not only protect ourselves but others as well.

God has not given us a spirit of fear so that we yield to the enemy and surrender. God has given us a spirit of power, of love, and of a sound mind.[18] He has given us power in the weapons of prayer and His word. He has given us love so that we not only fight for ourselves but for those around us, and He has given us a sound mind so that we are able to be aware of our surroundings, know our enemy, keep our mind and eyes on target, be ready for battle, and understand that in this war we fight against principalities, powers, and rulers of this dark age. We have been given armor—a sword and a bow—and told to stand against the enemy. Now, we must make that choice both for ourselves and for others.

# Being Bold

*"And for me, that utterance may be given to me, that I may open my mouth boldly to make known the mystery of the gospel, for which I am an ambassador in chains; that in it I may speak boldly, as I ought to speak."*
*- Ephesians 6:19-20*

Theo did not have the courage to fight the enemy alone, but the messenger encouraged him. Paul writes asking prayer for himself, so that he "may open [his] mouth boldly to make known the mystery of the gospel." He is an ambassador, a soldier for Christ bound in chains. Yet, he asks the saints in Ephesus for prayer that he may continue as he ought, fighting the spiritual battle and fulfilling his mission as a soldier of Christ with boldness. Bold is defined as not hesitating or fearful in the face of actual or possible danger but being courageous. Amid the battle, we face many challenges. We can become tired, overwhelmed, or scared. Theo was overwhelmed when he fought off an enemy only to be jumped by two more. He saw his opponents flood into his castle and was afraid. He became weary. But through it all the messenger encouraged Theo and told him not to fear. He encouraged him through the fight. This is what Paul asks from the believers in Ephesus. He asks for prayer of reinforcement and courage. Paul was imprisoned for Christ in Rome, and he was awaiting trial by Caesar. He could see the danger ahead of him. He knew fears would taunt him, but he also knew of the war surrounding him and the power of prayer.

## -Prayer Strengthens-

Prayer goes beyond ourselves. It is used to strengthen others. Paul knew the enemy would fight against the gospel and the truth, and he needed backup. He needed the encouragement to continue to fight the good fight. Even before Paul appealed to Caesar, God spoke to him and said, take courage; "as you have testified for Me in Jerusalem, so you must also bear witness at Rome."[1] Paul knew this battle would come. He was ready and willing to fight, but he asked his comrades, men in arms, for spiritual backup, for encouragement, for boldness. Even though Paul knew this was his fight, he still asked for prayer. He asked others to pray for boldness and courage in the fight ahead of him. He tells the Philippians, it is his "earnest expectation and hope that in nothing I shall be ashamed, but with all boldness, as always, so now also Christ will be magnified in my body, whether by life or by death."[2] Death should not be feared. As soldiers of Christ, our hope is in Christ Jesus; death cannot stop the goodness of God. He now lives forever, and He has made a way for us to live in eternity with Him. Death has no power, except as God allows. As soldiers, our desire should be to honor and glorify God, no matter what happens. Paul told Timothy that a good soldier does not entangle himself in the affairs of this life, but his aim is to "please him who enlisted him as a soldier."[3] As the messenger told Theo, "No matter what happens, I choose to stand and follow my King." No matter what happens, we fight, for the glory of God for the battle belongs to Him. Death cannot stop the victory.

## -Boldness Given-

This is not the first time that boldness has been prayed for or given in scripture. In the book of Judges, before Gideon fights the Midianites, the Lord gave him courage, telling him that if he was afraid, he should go to the camp and "hear what they say; and afterward your hands shall be strengthened."[4] God gave Gideon the courage and boldness needed. David proclaimed that "in the day I cried out, You answered me, and made me bold with strength in my soul."[5] The apostles also prayed for boldness. Peter and John faced the Sanhedrin and were warned not to talk or speak in the name of Jesus again, but they did not let the threats of men in this world stop them from obeying God. They prayed for boldness to continue the fight, to continue speaking the good news of Christ, and it was granted to them.[6] Shortly afterwards, the fight increased and persecution of the church began.[7] Many were imprisoned, tortured, or killed, but the fear of death and persecution did not stop them from fighting. As soldiers of Christ, they continued carrying out their orders. They were obedient to follow Christ no matter the cost. They continued to stand boldly for God, speaking the word of God and the truth of the resurrection. All the threats of the enemy would not stop them from carrying out the will of the Father. As Christian soldiers, it is important that we pray for boldness to continue the fight, so that we may face the coming threats and battles courageously and not fear. Are we willing to pray for boldness for ourselves and others, to stand against the threats and wiles of the enemy? We are like Theo: we have the armor and weapons needed for the fight, but now we need to stand strong, not falter, and remain fearless. We are not to be unwise in our courage, but bold in the fight where God calls us to stand.

We will face situations that cause fear. However, we must pray for boldness and keep our focus on God, "For He Himself has said, 'I will never leave you nor forsake you.' So we may boldly say: 'The Lord is my helper; I will not fear. What can man do to me?'"[8] Christ says, "do not worry about tomorrow, for tomorrow will worry about its own things. Sufficient for the day is its own trouble."[9] We are not to focus on the fear or worry of today and tomorrow, but we are to seek God, His Kingdom, and His righteousness. When Theo put aside the threat of the enemy, he stood firm and courageous as he faced the coming battle. He knew this fight was near, but scripture tells us, "Do not be overcome by evil, but overcome evil with good."[10] Christ has already conquered death, and He will conquer the enemy again in the end. But for now, we are to stand firm and boldly as soldiers of God.

# Choosing to Fight

*". . . And having done all, to stand." - Ephesians 6:13*

In the story, Theo had to make the decision to fight. The messenger had armed him for battle and instructed him, but he had to choose. In Ephesians six, Paul instructs us, "having done all," stand. He arms the soldiers of Christ to stand. But as Paul and the people in Ephesus had to make their own decisions, we, too, must choose. We must choose to put on each piece of armor. They do not magically appear on us. God provides them, but we must make the decision to dress for battle. Like Theo and the messenger dressed in their armor and prepared for battle, we also must make the effort and decision to take up the armor and stand against the enemy. This is a daily decision. Every day we choose: are we going to ignore the fight, surrender to the pressures and schemes of the enemy, or stand and fight?

## -Consequences-

Every choice has an action, and every action has a consequence. When Theo was entrusted with the castle, the enemy surrounded him. When the messenger and Theo stood their ground, the enemy attacked. When we enter the ranks of God's soldiers, the devil advances against us. When we stand in truth, he will strike at us. Some choices have detrimental consequences–like the man who let the enemy into the castle, or the man who surrendered and perished. Throughout the scriptures, God warns us that we will be judged according to our choices and actions. Paul writes in his letter to the Romans that God will "render to each one according to his deeds" and actions.[1] To those who do good, the spiritual consequences will be good. To those who do wrong, the spiritual consequence is punishment and death on Judgment Day. In Ezekiel, the people are complaining about how God's ways are not fair. Yet, it is *mankind's* ways that are not fair, because God is just. His ways are perfect. It is mankind that is imperfect and unjust. God's response to the people is that if a man does what is right, he will be saved, and if he turns away from the Lord, he will perish. The Lord says, "I will judge every one of you according to his own ways."[2] As a consequence for their actions, God said to Israel that He would "make the land desolate, because they ... persisted in unfaithfulness."[3] Yet, if they did right, He would bless them for generations. Our choices and actions have consequences. Do not indulge in the ways of the flesh or ponder the ways of the enemy, for we each "will give an account to Him who is ready to judge."[4] We see the consequence of our choices in Matthew: those who do the will of the Master enter the Kingdom, but those who choose to walk in their own will–in iniquity–do not enter the Kingdom. To those He will say, "I never knew you; depart from Me."[5] In scripture, there is a parable of a man and his three servants. He gave the first servant three talents, the second servant two talents, and the third servant one talent. Each talent equaled six hundred denarii, and a denarius equaled a normal day's wage. Then he goes on a long journey. While he is gone, two of the servants invest their money to please the master, but the third servant did not do as the master would have wanted. Instead, he did his own will and followed his own rationale and buried the money. When the master returned, he called his servants to stand before him and give an account for their stewardship of his money. The two who invested their money pleased the master and were told, "Well done, good and faithful servant." The third, who did not honor his master, was called a "wicked servant" and was cast out. Furthermore, what he had was taken from him and given to the first servant.[6] The servants' actions had consequences to match their choices. The wicked servant set his heart to do his own will and suffered the consequences. Yet, the two who set their hearts to do the master's will received a great reward.

Do not be deceived by the enemy or enticed by the lusts of the flesh. Fight the battle, listen to the Holy Spirit, and walk according to holiness. Joshua told the people of Israel to choose this day the God you will serve, "But as for me and my house, we will serve the LORD."[7] As the messenger asked Theo, "What will you choose?" We, too, must choose. Over and again, Paul instructs the soldiers of God with commands to: *put on, take up, stand, gird, shod, take,* and *pray*. He is giving us the choice. God has provided the weapons; we must decide to stand and fight.

We, as soldiers, are given a responsibility to look after and tend to what has been entrusted to us. Just as Theo was entrusted with the castle, we are given responsibility over our spiritual castles: our lives, our choices, and our actions. What we choose matters, and our choices will determine the direction of our lives. Theo's choice and actions impacted his entire life. He chose to answer the King's call and protect the castle. He chose to learn how to use his armor and sword. He chose to defend. These choices allowed him the ability to fight the enemy, and they brought good consequences. However, when he chose to give into the temptation of sleep, the consequence was painful and nearly deadly. At the end, he had to choose again if he would continue the fight or surrender to the pressure and will of the enemy. The men in the stories had the same decision to make, surrender or stand and fight. Each choice has a consequence. Some are detrimental and deadly. Others bring life, liberty, and victory, although we must fight for them. The same choices lie before us. Life and death are before you, "therefore chose life."[8] In the book of Deuteronomy, God tells the soldiers of Israel, "See, I have set before you today life and good, death and evil, in that I command you today to love the Lord your God, to walk in His ways, and to keep His commandments, His statues, and His judgments, that you may live. . . . But if your heart turns away so that you do not hear, and are drawn away . . . you shall surely perish. . . ."[9]

# -Consider Your Ways-

Before we act, we ought to take into consideration the possible consequences of our actions. In Scripture, the prophet Haggai tells us to "Consider [our] ways!"[10] In following Christ, we are instructed to count the cost of being His disciple.[11] Jesus said the world hates those who follow Him, but for those who follow and obey Him, He is the way, the truth, and the life.[12] Isaiah encourages the people, "This is the way, walk in it. . . ."[13] James tells us the consequence for sin is death.[14] This is not something to be taken lightly. A soldier must fight the enemies around him or be taken captive. There is no middle ground. From the beginning of creation, God has given mankind choices and consequences. So long as Adam and Eve obeyed and did not eat the fruit of the tree of good and evil, they were able to stay in the garden. But when they disobeyed, their consequence was death and banishment from the garden. Sin separated them from God. God told Cain, that if he did right, he would be accepted, but if he did *not* do right, sin crouched at his door waiting to devour him.[15] Cain had the opportunity to restrain sin, but he chose instead to let sin through the door. He chose to kill his brother. As his consequence, Cain was driven away, separated from all he knew.[16] In the book of Proverbs, Solomon warns us not to desire the things of the wicked, saying, "As righteousness leads to life, so he who pursues evil pursues it to his own death."[17]

In this spiritual battle, we all must choose where we will stand. There is only one side that wins in the end: Christ's. If we choose Christ, we are to follow Him no matter what. We lay aside "all filthiness and overflow of wickedness, and receive with meekness the implanted word, which is able to save [our] souls."[18] God has laid before us the consequences of both sides. Scripture tells us what happens to those who do not follow and love Christ: they will be cast out where there is weeping and gnashing of teeth,[19] where the fire never ends, and where the worm never stops eating.[20] But those who follow and love Christ will reign with Him in eternity;[21] they will receive a crown of glory;[22] their sorrows will be no more.[23] It is now our decision. Decide right now whom you will serve. There is no in-between. If we straddle the fence, we are like the church in Revelation who was neither hot nor cold and was spewed out of God's mouth.[24]

## -Choose-

We are called and chosen as God's soldiers in this spiritual battle against evil. Will we answer that call and put on the spiritual armor and take a stand? Satan, the enemy of our soul, wants us dead, and he makes war against us. Just as the enemy surrounded Theo's castle, the devil surrounds the camp of the saints.[25] We are in a spiritual war. The enemy beats against our walls. We must respond. The messenger asked Theo, "What will you choose?" It is now our turn—What will we choose? When we pledge our allegiance to Christ, and when we accept Him as our Lord, we become His. We enter the ranks of His soldiers. Immediately, He equips us with the armor and weapons for the battles ahead. He knows the fights we will encounter. He knows what is coming our way, and He gives us the weapons we need to win. Our lives as soldiers of Christ will not be easy.[26] There will be battles. We will have difficult and hard times. The world will hate us because it hates Him.[27] But do not to lose heart.[28] The victory is greater than the battle. Christ is coming, and He will conquer the enemy. It is as the messenger told Theo, the King "shall smite the foes, and they will kneel or die before him. Nothing can stand or prevail against the King." In Revelation, Christ comes on a white horse. He is called "Faithful and True, and in righteousness He judges and makes war."[29] When the enemy rises against Him, He will prevail, and "the devil, who deceived them," will be "cast into the lake of fire and brimstone."[30] In the end, victory belongs to the Lord, and those who are His will rejoice in it. Truly, what He has in store for us is better than anything we could imagine. As the messenger stood beside Theo, God the Holy Spirit stands beside us, encouraging us to stand strong and hold fast. The writer of the book of Hebrews proclaims, "Let us hold fast the confession of our hope without wavering, for He who promised is faithful."[31] God is faithful. He will never leave us.[32] He has prepared a way for us by sending His Son to die in our place for our mistakes. We can never win the war on our own. It is Christ in us who gives us power over the enemy. When Christ returns as King, the enemy will be defeated forever. If we stand with Christ and endure as good soldiers fighting the good fight of faith, then great is our reward in heaven. Victory over the enemy is certain through Christ Jesus our Lord. For God "has delivered us from the power of darkness and conveyed us into the kingdom of the Son of His love, in whom we have the redemption through His blood, the forgiveness of sins."[33]

If you do not know Christ, I pray you meet Him now. There is a battle going on, and Satan does not care who he kills in the process. He is after eternal destruction for humanity. Christ, on the other hand, wishes that none would perish.[34] He came to save the lost[35] and heal the brokenhearted,[36] to bind up, to mend, and to save. He wants all to come to know Him and live with Him for eternity. He cares for and loves us so much that He came to earth as a baby and died as a man paying the price for our sins. He suffered, bled, and died so we could live.[37] He rose again and is seated at the right hand of God.[38] He is preparing a place for those who accept His offer of salvation.[39] Over 2,000 years ago, Christ came, died, and rose from the dead so that we would have the choice, the opportunity, to live with Him throughout eternity. I pray that you make that decision right now and become a warrior and soldier for Christ.

May you not be overcome by evil, but may you overcome evil with good.[40] May the Lord bless you and keep you. May His face shine upon you, and be gracious to you and give you His peace.[41]

# Epilogue

The arrow struck the plank right outside the center. Theo drew another arrow, placed it in position, and released. Again, it struck near the center. A cluster of arrows marked his efforts from the last hour. He had risen before dawn to practice. *If I am to succeed in the battles ahead, I must stay ready.* He walked up to the plank to retrieve his collection of arrows.

"You are greatly improving yourself. I see you are up bright and early again today. Just as you have been for the last several days," the messenger said as he approached Theo.

"Yes. I do not want to be caught unaware again," Theo said, pulling the last arrow from the target. "I know more battles will come, and I want to be ready."

The messenger smiled and nodded. "Continue as you are, and you shall. Now, come. Walk with me to the gate."

As the two walked through the courtyard, the morning rays of sun shone before them. Shadows were driven away with each beam of light. Stones from the shattered wall were still scattered across the castle grounds. While evidence of the past struggle was present, there was a peaceful quiet that rested over the castle.

"What will you do now?" Theo asked as they approached the gate.

"If the King wills it," the messenger said, "I shall travel North and help another in need. War is ever around us."

"As I well know," Theo stated, looking at the damage. Broken arrows and pieces of enemy armor were stacked in a pile at the far entrance. The wall was slowly being rebuilt, and his wound, while healing, still had to be tended. The castle had suffered during the fight, but they had been victorious. Soldiers from the King of the Highlands arrived just in time and struck the enemy's army, causing them to run, abandoning their positions and the fight. The days that passed were full of soldiers hard at work repairing the damage. Some carried bricks and mortar to rebuild the wall. Others cleaned away the debris. Progress was evident, but they were not yet finished.

Surveying the work around them, the messenger placed a hand on Theo's shoulder. "Do not lose heart or be downcast. It will be strengthened."

Taking a deep breath, Theo asked, "What will happen the next time? I know they will come back again. You said yourself it never stops."

Smiling, the messenger said, "I have taught you the way. You have been given everything you need to stand strong. You have been instructed on how to use your weapons, and you have prevailed in this battle. There will be others, but do not fear them when they come. Continue to grow from them. The King of the Highlands is strengthening you with this task, so be strong and courageous. Do not fear, and do not stop fighting." Embracing him as a brother in arms, the messenger turned to go.

"Remember," he said. "You are never alone. I shall not be far off. And if you are ever in need, call on the King, and he will send help. Trust in him. He will never lead you astray." The messenger threw a brown traveler's sack over his shoulder and began to walk away. As he passed through the gate, he turned back. Lifting his hand in a wave, he prayed for Theo's steadfastness, that he would stand, endure, and remain strong in the battles ahead.

Theo waved back and returned to his practice and to rebuilding the wall.

Lifting his eyes, the messenger began his walk Northward. There was another soldier in need, another enemy to face, and another battle to fight.

# Acknowledgments

First, I want to acknowledge and thank God for His hand and direction in my life. Without His wisdom, instruction, and Holy Spirit guidance, this study would never have been completed or even started. God has shown and taught me many lessons while writing this book. I have experienced much of what I have described within its pages. Through it all, God reminded me of His goodness, authority, and power over the enemy. To God be the glory!

Additionally, this book would not be the same without the encouragement and help I received from others. A huge thank you belongs to both my parents. Thank you, Mom, for asking me if I were to write a study what would it be on and for being my constant editor through multiple drafts. Thank you, Dad, for teaching me that there is a spiritual battle mindset, for helping me to see the battles around me, and for instilling in me the importance of the armor of God. Thank you both for raising me the way you did. I cannot imagine a better place to grow up or better parents for the task.

Thank you to my siblings for all the prayers, encouragement, and reminders to finish.

Thank you to Joseph, Joshua, Justin, and Ray for reading and reviewing the early manuscript.

Thank you to Tommy Green for encouraging me to write the story, even though it took me a few years to finish it.

Thank you to Madison, who kept asking how it was coming along. God used you as a reminder to me to continue working and pressing forward with the writing process.

Thank you to Dolan Trout for designing the fantastic cover.

Thank you to all my friends who asked what I had been doing and for listening to my thoughts, explanations, or ideas about Theo and the study.

Thank you to Tara Johnson for all the help, advice, and encouragement.

Thank you to those I met at the Blue Lake Christian Writers Conference who encouraged me to write what God had given and instructed me to do.

Thank you to my editor, Michael White.

Thank you, reader, for taking time to experience Theo's story and the reflections of the armor of God. I hope and pray that you will use the armor God has equipped you with and that you will stand strong against the wiles of the enemy, for God has not given us a spirit of fear, but of power, and of love, and of a sound mind.

# About the Author

Charisa Hagel is first and foremost a Christian and child of the King. She believes that God has a purpose for everyone. This life may be full of trials, but God is always good, even when we cannot see it or understand it.

Charisa loves to read and write. She has always had an interest in writing and was awarded recognition for her short stories and poems. She has a heart for service and believes that serving others is a huge part of the Christian life. Charisa desires to strengthen those in the body of Christ to stand strong. She is also the co-director and co-founder of the Seasons Young Adult Conference, which ministers to those in their twenties and thirties.

Charisa resides in Alabama with her loving family. One of her favorite scripture verses is Philippians 1:20, which states, "according to my earnest expectation and hope that in nothing I shall be ashamed, but with all boldness, as always, so now also Christ will be magnified in my body, whether by life or by death."

To learn more about Charisa Hagel or to contact her, visit her website at www.hagelbooks.com.

# Endnotes

We are Chosen

1. Hebrews 13:5
2. 2 Corinthians 10:4
3. Revelation 12:7, Ephesians 6:12, Daniel 10:13, 20
4. Revelation 2 & 3
5. 1 Timothy 6:12
6. 1 Peter 2:9
7. 2 Timothy 2:22
8. 1 Peter 1:15-16, 2:5
9. 1 Peter 2:21
10. Philippians 3:17, 1 Corinthians 11:1
11. 2 Timothy 1:13
12. James 5:10
13. Matthew 25:24-25
14. John 17:21
15. John 14:6
16. John 5:39, John 8:55
17. John 14:7

18. Matthew 22:37-38

19. John 14:15

20. John 10:11-14

21. Hebrews 13:5

22. John 14:26

23. John 16:13

24. Proverbs 1:26

Be Strong

1. Matthew 19:26

2. Psalm 18:34

3. Psalm 32:8

4. 2 Samuel 22:40

5. Romans 8:31

6. James 4:7

7. Nehemiah 8:10

8. Psalm 27:1

9. Hebrews 12:2

10. Matthew 19:26, Mark 10:27, Luke 1:37

11. John 16:33

12. 2 Timothy 1:7

13. Job 1:21

14. 2 Timothy 2:4

15. Mark 12:30

16. Proverbs 3:5

Wiles of the Devil

1. Genesis 3:1-13

2. Genesis 4:7

3. 2 Corinthians 2:11

4. Exodus 14:10-13

5. Genesis 37:11, 18-22, 28

6. Exodus 2:11-14, Acts 7:23-25

7. Joshua 9:3-6, 14-15

8. Judges 16:15-21, 30

9. 2 Samuel 12:9-10, 14

10. 1 Kings 11:1-10

11. 1 Kings 12:26-31. 14:9-10

12. 2 Kings 5:20-27

13. Jonah 1:1-3

14. Mark 15:10, John 5:18, Matthew 26:3-4

15. John 6:53-60

16. John 19:12

17. Matthew 26:69-75

18. 2 Timothy 4:10

19. Acts 5:1-9

20. Genesis 2:15-17, 3:1-6

21. Numbers 14:40-45

22. 1 Samuel 15:18-26

23. 1 Samuel 15:22

24. Joshua 10:7-9

25. Judges 16:28-30

26. Psalm 51

27. Matthew 26:75, John 21:15-19

28. 1 Samuel 12:20-22

29. 1 Corinthians 10:13

## Physical and Spiritual Battles

1. Galatians 5:17, 1 Peter 2:11

2. 1 Kings 19:12

3. John 3:8

4. 2 Corinthians 10:5

5. Luke 22:42

6. Colossians 3:1, Romans 8:5

7. 1 Corinthians 9:27

8. Luke 12:48

9. Matthew 6:10

10. Daniel 10:12

11. Daniel 10:13, 20-21

12. Daniel 10:16

13. Daniel 10:18-19

14. 2 Kings 4:27

15. 2 Kings 6:15-16

16. 2 Kings 6:17

17. Proverbs 6:9

18. Proverbs 6:11

19. Romans 13:11-12

20. 1 Peter 2:9

21. John 8:12

22. Ephesians 5:8

23. Matthew 5:14

24. John 3:20

25. 1 Timothy 6:12

26. Ephesians 6:12

27. 2 Peter 3:9

Standing Ready

1. Colossians 3:5, Romans 8:13

2. Revelation 20:10

3. 2 Corinthians 10:5

4. Psalm 46:10

5. Philippians 4:11

6. 1 Corinthians 9:27

7. Matthew 6:34

8. Matthew 6:25-26

9. Exodus 14:13, Deuteronomy 3:22, 20:1-3, 31:6, Joshua 1:9, Isaiah 41:10, Psalm 56:4, Proverbs 3:25, Matthew 14:27, Luke 1:30, Revelation 1:17

10. 1 Peter 3:14

11. Ephesians 6:11, 13

12. John 10:10

13. Proverbs 24:16

14. James 4:7

15. Revelation 12:4, 7-9

16. Revelation 12:17

17. Mark 5:1-9

18. Job 1:7, 1 Peter 5:8, Revelation 12:9

19. John 16:33

20. Revelation 12:11

21. Psalm 27:3

22. 1 John 4:4

The Belt of Truth

1. Ephesians 6:14
2. John 14:6
3. John 8:44
4. Genesis 3:1
5. Genesis 3:6
6. Genesis 3:1
7. Genesis 3:15
8. Revelation 12:9
9. Genesis 3:1
10. Genesis 2:16-17
11. Genesis 3:2-3
12. Genesis 3:4
13. Genesis 3:5
14. Genesis 3:6
15. Matthew 4, Luke 4
16. Matthew 7:23
17. Matthew 13:42
18. Mark 9:44
19. 1 John 1:9

20. Romans 12:21

21. Matthew 4:4, 7, 10

22. Matthew 4:2

23. Numbers 11

24. Matthew 4:3

25. Mathew 4:4

26. Deuteronomy 8:3

27. Matthew 27:41-43

28. Luke 23:35

29. Revelation 13:8

30. Matthew 4:6

31. Matthew 4:7

32. Psalm 91:13

33. Colossians 2:10, 1 Corinthians 15:24-25

34. Luke 4:6

35. Revelation 12:9

36. Matthew 4: 10

37. Hebrews 12:1-2

38. James 4:7

39. Luke 4:13

40. Galatians 5:17, 1 Peter 2:11

41. 1 Peter 4:1-3

42. Psalm 18:34

43. Psalm 62:6

44. Isaiah 40:31

45. Galatians 5:24-25

46. Proverbs 24:16

47. 2 Thessalonians 3:13, Galatians 6:9

48. 1 Timothy 3:6

49. Proverbs 16:5

50. James 4:6

51. Matthew 6:22-23

52. Hebrews 4:15-16

53. 1 Peter 2:21

54. 1 Corinthians 11:1

55. Matthew 16:24

56. Proverbs 24:16

57. 2 Chronicles 7:14

58. Matthew 10:22

The Breastplate of Righteousness

1. Proverbs 17:22

2. Philippians 4:8

3. 2 Timothy 3:13-14

4. 2 Timothy 3:12

5. Luke 12:48

6. Philippians 2:14-16

7. Romans 12:21

8. Proverbs 4:23

9. Hebrews 12:1

10. Proverbs 3:5

11. Jeremiah 29:11

12. 2 Timothy 2:4

13. 1 John 1:5-10, 2:3-6, 15

14. James 4:4

15. 1 John 2:15

16. James 4:1-10, Mark 13:13

17. John 17

18. 1 John 2

19. 1 John 2:29

20. Matthew 7:23

21. Matthew 5:16

22. Philippians 2:5-8

23. 1 John 3:11, 1 Corinthians 13:4-6, Ephesians 5:2

24. Philippians 2:8, John 14:15

25. Romans 12:9

26. 2 Timothy 2:22

27. 1 John 3:3

28. Matthew 20:25-28

29. Galatians 5:22-23

30. Galatians 5:16

31. Galatians 5:24-25

32. Romans 12:2

33. Matthew 6:25-34

34. Romans 14:17

35. John 14:27

36. John 14:26

37. Micah 6:8

38. Colossians 3:2

39. Colossians 1:21-22

40. Proverbs 17:3, 1 Thessalonians 2:4

41. Acts 13:22

42. 1 Samuel 16:7

43. Matthew 15:11

44. Psalm 51:10

45. Psalm 139:23-24

46. Matthew 12:33

47. Matthew 7:17

48. 1 John 2:29, 3:10

49. 1 Peter 2:1, Colossians 3:5, 8-9

50. John 8:37-47, 54-56

51. Matthew 23:28

52. 1 John 3:12

53. Genesis 7:1, Hebrews 11:7

54. James 2:23

55. Acts 4:13

56. 2 Corinthains 4:9

57. Revelation 3:2

The Shoes of Preparation and Peace

1. Philippians 4:7

2. Isaiah 26:3

3. 2 Samuel 23:11-12

4. 2 Timothy 1:7

5. John 2:17

6. John 14:27

7. John 19:12

8. John 19:4, 6

9. Acts 4:13-21

10. 2 Timothy 4:4

11. Ezekiel 13:10

12. Isaiah 59:8

13. John 15:19, Luke 21:12

14. John 15:20

15. Matthew 5:10-12

16. 2 Timothy 3:12

17. *Foxe's Book of Martyrs*

18. Philippians 1:21

19. Acts 14:22

20. Matthew 10:38

21. Matthew 10:28, Luke 12:4-5

22. Psalm 23:2-5

23. Philippians 4:7

24. Acts 16:25

25. Acts 16:26

26. 1 Kings 18:20-40

27. 1 Kings 19:2

28. 1 Kings 19:3

29. 1 Kings 19:4

30. 1 Kings 19:5-8

31. Colossians 3:15

32. Psalm 27:14

33. Psalm 23:3

34. Psalm 18:2

35. 1 Corinthians 15:57

The Shield of Faith

1. Psalm 18:30

2. 1 Samuel 13:22

3. 1 Samuel 14:6

4. Luke 10:1

5. Acts 3:1-6, 11-12

6. Acts 13, 15:25, 40

7. Philippians 2:19-30, Philemon

8. 1 Corinthians 16:13

9. 2 Timothy 1:7

10. 1 Peter 5:9

11. Hebrews 11:1

12. Luke 12:48

13. Psalm 3:3

14. 2 Samuel 22:35

15. 2 Corinthians 12:9

16. 2 Corinthians 12:10

17. Hebrews 13:5

18. Hebrews 11:33-34

19. Judges 6:11-14

20. Judges 7:7

21. Judges 7:12

22. Zechariah 4:6

23. Judges 7:15

24. 1 John 4:4

25. James 2:20

26. Acts 5:1-11

27. Acts 5:3

28. 2 Timothy 4:10

29. Luke 22:54-62

30. 2 Timothy 4:7

31. 2 Corinthians 11:24-27

The Helmet of Salvation

1. Joshua 24:15

2. Matthew 12:43-44

3. Matthew 12:44-45
4. Colossians 3:2
5. Mark 8:33
6. Psalm 37:39
7. 2 Corinthians 10:3
8. Ephesians 6:12
9. 2 Corinthians 10:4-6
10. 1 Samuel 17:47
11. Proverbs 21:31
12. Psalm 27:1
13. Exodus 20:3
14. Matthew 11:15, 13:9, 43, Mark 4:9, 23, 7:16
15. Hebrews 13:5
16. Ezekiel 12
17. Romans 15:5-6, Philippians 2:1-7
18. Philippians 2:8
19. Acts 19:13-17
20. Proverbs 21:31
21. John 10:10
22. 2 Peter 3:9
23. John 14:6

24. James 2:7

25. Acts 7:52

26. 1 John 3:3

27. John 15:13

28. John 3:16

29. 1 John 4:8

30. Romans 6:1-2

31. 1 Chronicles 28:9

The Sword of The Spirit

1. Acts 14:19

2. Acts 14:20

3. Judges 7:5

4. Judges 7:7

5. John 10:10

6. 1 John 4:1

7. Joshua 9:4-9

8. Proverbs 16:2

9. Proverbs 21:2, 24:12

10. Jeremiah 17:10

11. Hebrews 4:12

12. 1 Thessalonians 2:4

13. Revelation 2:23

14. Jeremiah 17:9

15. 2 Corinthians 11:14

16. Revelation 12:9

17. 1 Peter 5:8, John 8:44

18. Hebrews 4:12

19. Isaiah 54:17

20. 1 John 4:4

21. Galatians 2:20

22. John 14:12

23. James 4:7-8

24. Isaiah 55:11

25. Exodus 3:7-8, 10

26. Exodus 3:12

27. Exodus 4:14-16

28. Exodus 4:2

29. Exodus 4:17

30. 2 Corinthians 6:16

31. 2 Timothy 2:3-4

32. Joel 2:5

33. Joel 2:11

34. Joshua 5:13

35. Joshua 5:14

36. Numbers 22:31

37. 1 Chronicles 21:16

38. 1 Chronicles 21:30

39. Joel 3:9

40. Judges 7:20

41. Deuteronomy 33:29

42. Matthew 4:1-11

43. Deuteronomy 30:14

44. 2 Timothy 3:16-17

45. Judges 6:11-14

46. Hebrews 11:7

47. Hebrews 11:34

48. Hebrews 13:8

49. John 14:26

50. Mark 13:11

51. Hebrews 4:12

52. Romans 12:21

53. Jude 1:9

54. Zechariah 3:2

55. Acts 19:15-16

56. Mark 16:17

57. Acts 16:18

58. Revelation 12:11

59. Luke 4:1-13

60. Revelation 20:3

61. Psalm 27:3,13

62. Romans 8:28

63. 2 Peter 3:9

64. Exodus 34:6, 2 Peter 3:9

65. Acts 1:7

66. Revelation 17:14, 1 Corinthians 15:26

67. 2 Chronicles 20:12

68. Romans 8:31

Praying Always

1. Luke 19:46

2. James 5:16

3. James 4:6

4. Matthew 5:24

5. Proverbs 15:29

6. Proverbs 28:9

7. Ecclesiastes 3:8

8. 2 Timothy 4:2

9. 1 Peter 5:8

10. Matthew 26:38

11. Matthew 26:41

12. Daniel 2:3-10

13. Daniel 2:16

14. Daniel 2:18

15. Revelation 1:11

16. Revelation 2:7, 11, 17, 29, 3:6, 13, 22

17. Matthew 26:41

18. 2 Timothy 1:7

Being Bold

1. Acts 23:11

2. Philippians 1:20

3. 2 Timothy 2:4

4. Judges 7:11

5. Psalm 138:3

6. Acts 4:29-31

7. Acts 8:1

8. Hebrews 13:5-6

9. Matthew 6:34

10. Romans 12:21

Choosing to Fight

1. Romans 2:6

2. Ezekiel 33:20

3. Ezekiel 15:8

4. 1 Peter 4:5

5. Matthew 7:23

6. Matthew 25:14-30

7. Joshua 24:15

8. Deuteronomy 30:19

9. Deuteronomy 30:15-18

10. Haggai 1:5, 7

11. Matthew 8:18-22, Luke 14:25-33

12. John 14:6

13. Isaiah 30:21

14. James 1:15

15. Genesis 4:7

16. Genesis 4:14

17. Proverbs 11:19

18. James 1:21

19. Matthew 25:30

20. Mark 9:43-44

21. Revelation 20:6

22. 1 Peter 5:4

23. Revelation 21:4

24. Revelation 3:16

25. Revelation 20:9

26. John 16:33, 2 Timothy 3:12, Luke 14:27, 33

27. John 15:18

28. 2 Corinthians 4:16, Galatians 6:9

29. Revelation 19:11

30. Revelation 20:10

31. Hebrews 10:23

32. Hebrews 13:5

33. Colossians 1:13-14

34. 2 Peter 3:9

35. Matthew 18:11, Luke 19:10

36. Psalm 147:3, Luke 4:18

37. Romans 5:8, Colossians 1:14

38. Ephesians 1:20

39. John 14:2-3

40. Romans 12:21

41. Numbers 6:24-25

www.ingramcontent.com/pod-product-compliance
Lightning Source LLC
Chambersburg PA
CBHW020851160426
43192CB00007B/878